PREVIEW GUIDE

Business Communication

15e

Business Communication

15e

Carol M. Lehman
Professor of Management
Mississippi State University

Debbie D. Dufrene
Professor of General Business
Stephen F. Austin State University

THOMSON
SOUTH-WESTERN

Australia · Brazil · Canada · Mexico · Singapore · Spain · United Kingdom · United States

THOMSON

SOUTH-WESTERN

Business Communication Preview Guide, Fifteenth Edition
Carol M. Lehman, Debbie D. DuFrene

VP/Editorial Director:
Jack W. Calhoun

Publisher:
Neil Marquardt

Acquisitions Editor:
Erin Joyner

Developmental Editor:
Katie Yanos

Marketing Manager:
Nicole Moore

Content Project Manager:
Darrell E. Frye

Manager of Technology, Editorial:
John Barans

Technology Project Editor:
John Rich

Manufacturing Coordinator:
Diane Gibbons

Art Director:
Stacy Jenkins Shirley

Production House:
LEAP Publishing Services, Inc.

Compositor:
International Typesetting and Composition

Printer:
Courier
Kendallville, Indiana

Internal and Cover Designer:
Ke Design

Cover Images:
© Getty Images and © Alamy

For more information about our products, contact us at:

Thomson Learning Academic Resource Center

1-800-423-0563

Thomson Higher Education
5191 Natorp Boulevard
Mason, OH 45040
USA

Brief Contents

1 Communication Foundations

2 Communication Analysis

3 Communicating Through Voice, Electronic and Written Messages

4 Communication Through Reports and Business Presentations

5 Communication for Employment

Contents

Part 2 *Communication Analysis* 71

3 Planning Spoken and Written Messages   72

4 Preparing Spoken and Written Messages

Part 3 *Communicating Through Voice, Electronic and Written Messages*

5 Communicating Electronically

8 Delivering Persuasive Messages

Part 4 *Communication Through Reports and Business Presentations*

9 Understanding the Report Process and Research Methods

Part 5 Communication for Employment

Preface

As professors of business communication, we understand expanding course content, changing learner characteristics, increased importance of assessment, and ever-changing technology needs. *Business Communication, 15e,* is a dynamic reflection of our response to changing expectations in the business communication course. Over six decades of use, *Business Communication* has established itself as the authoritative standard in the field. Not merely changing with the times but pushing the boundaries of change, this text continues to lead the pack in product innovation. *Business Communication, 15e,* pushes the boundaries once again, with a new look and feel—a compact text that offers the following learning assets in traditional and distance learning environments:

- Clear, comprehensive coverage of key content areas, including a self-contained team training guide, presented in 14 streamlined chapters that correspond well with the weeks in a typical semester.

- Problem solving with real-world cases, applications, and video segments that prepare students to speak, write, research, and collaborate proficiently using a wide array of communication technologies.

- A wealth of *expanded* web enrichment and *new* self-assessment measures.

- A learner-centered format that engages students and effectively links text and web.

We're eager for you to take a closer look at how *Business Communication, 15e,* is "Leading the Way" with an innovative text that is

L earner inspired

E mphasis rich

A ssessment driven

D esigner oriented

Learner-Inspired Pedagogy

As experienced professors in AACSB-accredited colleges of business, both of us know that today's learners have specific needs and preferred styles for acquiring knowledge and solving problems. Based on our extensive research of cognitive learning styles and technology assisted learning, *Business Communication, 15e,* offers a unique information delivery system that will involve your students in a more active way in text content and integrates text and web into a seamless unit.

New "Your Turn" Feature

Chapter content is "chunked" with interactive points for student involvement. Chapter reading becomes interactive, as the student encounters frequent "Your

Turn" opportunities to apply, practice, and assess learning. The following five "Your Turn" elements in each chapter draw the student into active learning.

Miscue

Miscommunications occur in the real world, often with embarrassment or even disastrous results. The Miscue feature in each chapter enforces the seriousness of these occurrences and asks students to think about prevention strategies. See the Visual Preface for "Miscue" examples.

You're the Professional

Students find themselves in the driver's seat as they justify their responses to a variety of business scenarios. Is it ethical to . . . . ? Should. . . . ? What about . . . ? See the Visual Preface for samples.

Career Portfolio

Documenting one's communication abilities is becoming more important to the hiring process as employers look for evidence beyond the résumé. The Career Portfolio feature guides students through the creation of various documents that illustrate their business communication competencies. View a Career Portfolio "Your Turn" on page 00 and another in the Visual Preface.

Assessment

Instructors, institutions, and accrediting bodies want to know that students have achieved course objectives. Each Assessment "Your Turn" is designed to reflect student knowledge and application of a core course concept, including cultural awareness, understanding of technology, ethical thinking, and various other essential areas. The Visual Preface illustrated an Assessment "Your Turn."

Electronic Café

Technology is integral in business communication course content. Electronic Cafes enable students to use various technologies to apply their understanding of key technology topics such as instant and text messaging, discussion boards, intranets, and web pages. See the Visual Preface for examples.

Sound Instructional Design

As in previous editions, *Business Communication* models the concise, coherent writing style demanded in business today. Revisions in the 15e apply cognitive theory principles to maximize learning and minimize the mental effort students must expend to process information. For example, note the following text example of a visual that combats cognitive overload and draws students to an appealing image integrated with key concepts in one convenient location. See for yourself the appealing streamlined format (less reading for your students) and increased learning potential achieved through integrated visuals:

- Channels of communication integrates an analysis of the available channels and memorable graphics.

- Level of formality required by various technologies compares and contrasts the writing style and format of various electronic communication channels.

- Good and poor examples of a persuasive message include a concise explanation of communication theory applied.

Redesigned PowerPoint slides require students to use both visual and auditory sensory channels to access essential information. While viewing the slides and listening to your lecture or the narration available with the lecture slides, students can maximize their learning of key chapter concepts.

Figure 1-2 Channels of Communication

Real-World Focus

A variety of cases and applications in every chapter capture student interest by bringing real-world organizations and successful professionals into the discussion of communication principles and practices.

- **Organizational Showcase.** Each chapter showcases the communication strategies of a real-world successful organization and provides users with an in-depth, multi-part experience. The chapter opens with an organizational response to a contemporary communication issue, continues with highlights of the communication strategies of a professional affiliated with the organization, and ends with a case providing further exploration and application of concepts that lead to success in the featured organization. In the 15th edition, you'll learn how eBay connects worldwide markets (Chapter 2), how the Sago Mine tragedy illustrates difficulties in sharing bad news (Chapter 7), how research and development strategies have been revolutionary for Apple (Chapter 9), and many more.

- **Real-World Applications.** Extended cases at the end of selected chapters are based on actual events and problems faced by real organizations. Students are asked, for instance, to consider the challenges associated with crisis communication through cases related to the Hurricane Katrina aftermath. An abundance of internal photos entice students to consider how communication effectiveness relates to contemporary events and issues. Many of these images draw students' attention to bonus content available at the text support site, such as the Janet Jackson and Justin Timberlake photo that refers students to the web for more information on apologies.

Emphasis-Rich Approach

Whatever the emphasis of your course, you'll find a wealth of resources in the text and technology package to support you, such as the following features:

Strategic Forces Model

A keystone since the 12th edition, the Strategic Forces model introduced in Chapter 1 and integrated through all remaining chapters makes it easy to weave contemporary topics into traditional subject matter, enforcing the impact that each has on effective business communication. The strategic model reflects four forces that have an inherent impact on business communication effectiveness: diversity, legal and ethics issues, technology, and the team environment. Students who understand the interrelationships of this model will be able to analyze business communication situations and design effective workplace communications. Two strategic feature boxes in each chapter and the Case Analysis, an extended case positioned at the end of the chapter, address pertinent strategic forces. Distinctive margin icons focus students' attention on the relevant strategic force. You can grasp the depth of coverage by reviewing the integration grid printed on the inside back cover of your text and reviewing the samples pages illustrated in the Visual Preface.

Sound Communication Pedagogy

The integration of written and spoken communication concepts throughout the text prepares students for communicating expertly through an ever-expanding number of channels. The annotated visual in Figure 6-1 reinforces the concept that communication involves a variety of spoken, electronic, and written messages. An updated Chapter 5, "Communicating Electronically," includes new coverage on writing for blogs, text messaging, and cautions related to the use of social networking Web sites. Numerous poor and good examples illustrate communication related to a variety of print and electronic documents.

Also, end-of-chapter activities and cases tabs are arranged for focus on the important skill areas of Reading, Thinking, Writing, Speaking, and Collaborating.

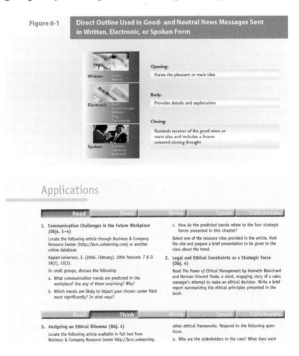

Technology

Technology coverage is contemporary—including the uses in business communication of instant messaging, blogging, and text messaging.

Team Development

As one of the strategic forces influencing business communication, team environment is an integral part of the 15th edition. Students learn about the importance of team skills and strategies for maximizing group effectiveness in Chapters 1 and 2. Strategic forces feature boxes address team writing skills, technologies that support collaborative skills, team interviews, and more. A team training guide, *Building High-Performance Teams*, packaged with each new copy of the 15th edition, offers groups a guided process for advancing through the various stages of team development and acquiring essential skills for a team-oriented workplace. Each of five projects provides students an opportunity for exploring, applying, and reflecting on key team skills. Sample team documents in the handbook and online templates give students a head start for effective team development within student teams.

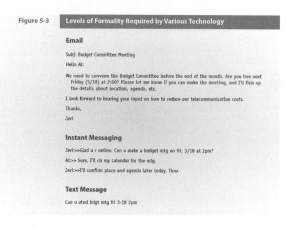

Figure 5-3 | Levels of Formality Required by Various Technology

Email

Subj: Budget Committee Meeting

Hello Al:

We need to convene the Budget Committee before the end of the month. Are you free next Friday (3/18) at 2:00? Please let me know if you can make the meeting, and I'll firm up the details about location, agenda, etc.

I look forward to hearing your input on how to reduce our telecommunication costs.

Thanks,

Jeri

Instant Messaging

Jeri:>>Glad u r online. Can u make a budget mtg on fri, 3/18 at 2pm?

Al:>> Sure, I'll clr my calendar for the mtg.

Jeri:>>I'll confirm place and agenda later today. Thnx

Text Message

Can u atnd bdgt mtg fri 3-18 2pm

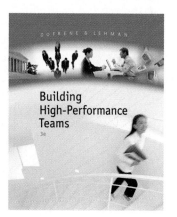

Assessment Driven Framework

A cadre of assessment tools responds to the current surge in requirements for assessment from regional accreditation bodies, the AACSB, and other agencies.

- A course pretest and posttest help you establish students' progress over the term.

- Online quizzes and assessments are available for each chapter through the ThomsonNOW product, by which students can measure and track their progress and receive feedback for improvement. Learn more about assessment tools available with ThomsonNow on page xxix.

- The text support site offers numerous assessment opportunities that allow students to email results to their instructor. Review these assessment tools at http://www.thomsonedu.com/bcomm/lehman.

- The text itself offers a variety of assessment measures as illustrated in the Visual Preface:

  - A vast array of assessment tools suited for your students appears at the end of each chapter.

  - The "Your Turn: Assessment" feature guides students in assessing a critical communication area. Students assess cultural awareness (Chapter 1), writing anxiety in Chapter 4, ethics in Chapter 8, and plagiarism in Chapter 9, and others. At the end of the term, students may present summary results of the 14 communication assessments to support their learning in the course.

- The "Your Turn: Career Portfolio" feature directs students in creating a representative set of documents they can use to showcase their communication skills for evaluation or employment.

Designer-Oriented Philosophy

With *Business Communication, 15e*, you can have it your way. Whether your course is online, hybrid, or face to face, *Business Communication* can be customized to meet the unique needs of your course and students.

The text is available in traditional bound print, looseleaf, and digital formats. Your book can also be customized to include just the chapters you teach. Available supplements include:

- *Building High-Performance Teams* handbook, designed to guide students easily through the team process.

- ThomsonNOW is the only web-based course management tool developed and tested by instructors to closely mirror each aspect of the teaching workflow, enhance student performance, and save instructors hours of time. It can be easily integrated into the instructor's course presentation or used by students without instructor involvement.

- Business & Company Resource Center (BCRC) that provides free access to a premier online business research tool for completing text assignments and cases. Your students can conveniently search the latest issues of respected business periodicals, as well as financial information, industry reports, and company histories.

- Free text support site with enrichment content to supplement text coverage, interactive chapter quizzes and language tutorial, convenient download of PowerPoint slides and assignment templates, up-to-date links to web resources, more model documents, GMAT writing tips, and much more.

- An alternate MLA reference style appendix that is available online and can be included in your customized print text.

About the Author Team

Both of us are professors in AACSB-accredited schools of business, each with more than twenty years' experience teaching business communication in traditional and distance classes. Actively engaged in research, we are frequent presenters at national and regional meetings of the Association for Business Communication, for which we sponsor the Meada Gibbs Outstanding Teacher Award. Our recent research on cognitive theory and technology-mediated learning reflect our commitment to identifying factors that affect the successful implementation of educational technology. This research has provided direction

Now it's your turn...

It's a pleasure to present *Business Communication* 15e, and to "lead the way" with a learning experience designed to prepare our students and yours for today's dynamic workplace. Best wishes for a rewarding course as you guide your students in reaching their career potential through effective communication. Please contact us or visit us at upcoming business communication conferences to share your comments, questions, and successes as we work together to prepare our students to become powerful communicators.

Debbie D. DuFrene   *Carol M. Lehman*

in designing a textbook and a technology-mediated learning package that is easy to use and directly related to course outcomes—instruction that is worthy of your and your students' time and money. You are encouraged to access the "Author" link at the text support site for more detailed information about us.

Leading the Way with Exceptional Instructor's Resources

A total package of instructional resources complements the *Business Communication, 15e,* to make your planning and presentation easier and more effective and to simplify and strengthen the study of business communication for your students. To provide you with relevant and timely resources, Carol Lehman and Debbie DuFrene are actively involved in the development of the supplemental elements and work daily with business communication educators who are carefully chosen to create various components.

Instructor's Resource CD

Provides convenient, one-stop access to the wide assortment of instructional resources supporting the 15e. Browse through the easy-to-navigate menu to view them all:

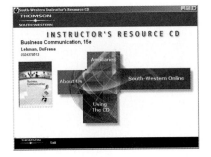

ThomsonNow Product

Need a brief description of the support that will be provided on the IRCD for this product.

Instructor's Resource Guide

The *Instructor's Resource Guide* organizes each chapter by learning objectives and includes a gold mine of teaching suggestions conveniently integrated with handy thumbnails of the PowerPoint slides and answers to chapter activities. Practical advice is provided for employing the text's distinctive features, teaching business communication in various formats, and assessing learning.

Test Bank

The *Test Bank* contains approximately 1,000 questions, 25 percent of which are new to the 15e. More higher-level questions have been added, along with applications requiring students to practice critical-thinking skills as they apply chapter concepts. A table at the beginning of each chapter classifies each question according to learning objective, type, and level of difficulty for easy selection.

ExamView Testing Software

The entire *Test Bank* is available electronically via ExamView on the Instructor's Resource CD. Instructors can create custom exams by selecting questions, editing existing questions, and adding new questions. Instructors can also have exams created by calling Thomson Learning's Academic Resource Center at 1-800-423-0563 (8:30 a.m. to 6 p.m. EST.)

PowerPoint Lecture and Resource Slides

PowerPoint resource slides provide supplementary information, activities to reinforce key concepts, and solutions to end-of-chapter activities. Students can view the lecture slides on the Web and print copies for taking notes or listen to the narrated version available with the ThomsonNow product.

Instructor Web Site

This robust password-protected teaching/learning center provides innovative teaching suggestions for traditional and distance delivery, assessment guidelines, GMAT applications, supplementary case problems, and much more. Go to www. thomsonedu.com/bcomm/lehman for more details about these comprehensive classroom resources.

ThomsonNow

The vast instructional benefits of this revolutionary product are illustrated on page xxi–xxx of this Preface.

Acknowledgments

Business Communication and its numerous support tools reflect the contributions of many talented people. These appreciated individuals include our faculty colleagues, our students at Mississippi State and Stephen F. Austin who have participated in our research studies and field tested our ideas, the publishing team at Thomson, and the many professional educators whose insightful reviews have been essential to the development of each edition of *Business Communication*. In response to an online survey, nearly 500 business communication instructors provided a wealth of constructive comments related to their preferences for topic coverage, focus, page length, and delivery options that aided us in identifying the wide range of needs, especially for those teaching business communication by distance. For their insights and suggestions, we extend sincere thanks to those completing the survey and the following reviewers of the 15e:

Heather J. Allman, University of West Florida
Debra Burleson, Baylor University
Lajuan Davis, University of Southern Mississippi
Sibylle Mabry, Louisiana State University
Jeanette S. Martin, University of Mississippi
Stephen J. Resch, Indiana Wesleyan University
Robert von der Osten, Ferris State University
Bennie J. Wilson III, University of Texas at San Antonio
Robert Yamaguchi, Fullerton College

For their constructive comments on *Building High-Performance Teams, 2nd edition*, we're grateful to the following reviewers:

Terrie Baumgardner, Pennsylvania State University
Priscilla Berry, Jacksonville University
Lana Carnes, Eastern Kentucky University
Bobbie Krapels, University of Mississippi
Jere' Littlejohn, University of Mississippi
David Rudnick, Hillsborough Community College
Christine Pye, California Lutheran University
Sharon E. Rouse, University of Southern Mississippi
Steven Austin Stovall, Wilmington College

Deepest appreciation goes to the following committed and talented business communication educators who worked closely with us to plan and develop important components of the comprehensive 15e package:

Judith Biss, Stephen F. Austin, Mississippi State University (*assessment content including the Test Bank, ThomsonNOW quiz elements, and selected cases*)
Denise Cosper, Mississippi State University (*PowerPoint slides, Instructor's Resource Guide, and selected cases*)

Gratitude is also extended to our devoted spouses who have supported us through this lengthy and demanding project, as well as to our college-age children who served as a convenient focus group for content issues and technology design.

LEHMAN & DUFRENE

Business Communication 15e

Pushing the Boundaries of Change

Over the past six decades, *Business Communication* has established itself as the authoritative standard in the field. Marked by a concise, coherent writing style, enriched with an abundance of model documents, and organized around a unique and effective Strategic Forces Model that translates communication theory into applied best practices, the text has consistently proven its value to both instructors and students.

This new edition is a dynamic response to changing expectations in both the business communication course and the workplace. The learner-centered format and new features of this edition effectively link the text with the latest teaching and learning technologies.

- **New "Your Turn" elements** in each chapter provide opportunities to apply, practice and assess communication skills
- **All new video cases** teach key concepts through real-world experience
- **The revolutionary ThomsonNOW™** product supports learning with expanded web enrichment

Strategic Forces Model Links Theory to Best Practices

The Strategic Forces Model is a lens through which students can view communications as a tool to help them create effective workplace communications. A keystone since the 12th edition, the Strategic Forces Model, introduced in Chapter 1 and integrated throughout all chapters, organizes content along four key forces that impact business communication effectiveness:

- **Changing technology**
- **Team environment**
- **Legal and ethical issues**
- **Diversity**

Students who understand the interrelationships of this model, and how it affects communication, can successfully analyze business communication situations and communicate expertly through an ever-expanding number of options—from traditional paper documents to e-mail, instant messaging, web communications, voice and wireless technologies, to whatever the future of technology holds!

Changing Technology

Business Communication, 15e is completely updated with in-depth coverage of the latest communication technology, including instant and text messaging, blogging, and social networking. **Your Turn** features let students explore the power and consequences of electronic communications.

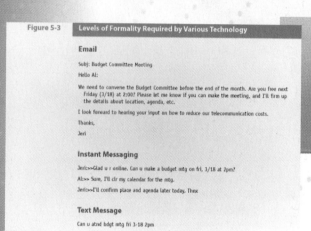

Figure 5-3 | **Levels of Formality Required by Various Technology**

Email

Subj: Budget Committee Meeting

Hello Al:

We need to convene the Budget Committee before the end of the month. Are you free next Friday (3/18) at 2:00? Please let me know if you can make the meeting, and I'll firm up the details about location, agenda, etc.

I look forward to hearing your input on how to reduce our telecommunication costs.

Thanks,

Jeri

Instant Messaging

Jeri:>>Glad u r online. Can u make a budget mtg on fri, 3/18 at 2pm?

Al:>> Sure, I'll clr my calendar for the mtg.

Jeri:>>I'll confirm place and agenda later today. Thnx

Text Message

Can u atnd bdgt mtg fri 3-18 2pm

5-5 your turn MISCUE

Matthew Brown, a Starbucks employee, was terminated from his job because of profanity-laced remarks he made about a manager and the company on his blog. Brown said he didn't use his real name and gave the blog address to a select group of people, so he doesn't know how the diary ended up in Starbucks' hands. While the blog was not easy to find, postings are permanently archived on the Internet. The derogatory posting violated the contract Starbucks employees sign agreeing not to make negative comments about the company.[17]

1. Do you know of a similar faux pas related to blogging? What were the consequences?
2. What advice would you give to a coworker who plans to start a blog?

DUFRENE & LEHMAN

Building High-Performance Teams

3e

Teams

Recognizing the dominance of the team environment in today's workplace, Lehman and DuFrene put heavy emphasis on learning team skills and strategies for maximizing group effectiveness. Strategic Forces boxes address team writing skills, team interviews, and technologies that support collaborative skills. A team training guide, ***Building High Performance Teams***, packaged with each new copy of *Business Communication, 15e*, provides advanced instruction and application of essential team-building skills.

STRATEGIC FORCES

Using Collaborative Technologies to Support Work Teams

New systems and workgroup software are bringing team members together and allowing them to share data on a timely basis no matter where they are located. Teams are able to reach better and faster decisions because they have the necessary information and the forum to participate in discussion and idea exchange. Work-group computing or collaborative computing are other terms used to describe this cooperative computing environment.

Leading collaboration software includes Lotus Notes and Domino software from IBM's Lotus Software Group and Microsoft Exchange Titanium. Electronic collaboration tools aid effective communication, collaboration, and coordination, especially in groups that are geographically dispersed. Productivity enhancements result because groupware offers the following advantages:[20]

- *A shared work area for teams to keep track of projects.* Up-to-date information can be accessed quickly and securely by everyone simultaneously. This "knowledge base" enables companies to respond quickly to customer needs and to new market opportunities.

- *Bulletin boards for discussing ideas, sharing and editing documents, and obtaining team member approval.* Bulletin board comments and questions are posted, stored, routed, and

accessed and reviewed quickly when a decision must be made. Rather than call a hurried meeting to ask a question or make an important announcement, teams can access and respond to a posted message and spend the saved time completing critical tasks.

- *Advance real-time communication.* Participants can be linked

together to read and respond to information on their computer screens, to participate in brainstorming sessions, and to vote on issues anonymously. Users in different locations can work simultaneously on the same documents on their screens and can hold a face-to-face meeting if videoconferencing technology is available.

- *Group calendar and scheduling.* The software identifies a

meeting, detects scheduling conflicts, and can even locate a member when needed. Success is dependent on the team's commitment to maintaining a complete and accurate calendar and concern for privacy.

- *Monitoring the flow of the team's work.* The software helps track the status of documents—who has them, who is behind schedule, and who gets the document next.

To achieve optimal results from collaborative software, employees need training in the technology, but more importantly they must learn to work collaboratively. They need a clear understanding of their roles and responsibilities so members can reach agreement and support others in the work to be done. Employees must also be committed to sharing information, files, and resources freely, with respect for confidentiality when appropriate—a concept in direct opposition to the traditional view that "knowledge is power." Visit the text support site to learn more about ways for developing people to work with collaborative technologies.

Application

From library research or your own networking activities, identify an organization that uses workgroup software for authoring and editing documents. Conduct an interview with a member of a collaborative team within the organization that seeks the following information: (1) software product used for collaborative writing, (2) number and expertise of colleagues who typically collaborate on a single document, and (3) reactions to the use of collaborative software in terms of advantages and disadvantages. Present the results of your interview in written or spoken

TEAM ENVIRONMENT

1-5 your turn Electronic Café

Instant Messaging Joins the Workforce

Instant messaging (IM) is not just for the younger set and their social conversations. Many firms are adopting instant messaging as a legitimate and valuable business tool. About a quarter of U.S. companies use IM as an official corporate communication service, and an additional 44 percent have employees who use IM on their own.[28] In thousands of organizations, instant messaging is complementing and replacing existing media such as email and voice messages. Some corporate leaders, however, have expressed concerns over productivity and security that might be jeopardized when using IM. The following electronic activities will allow you to explore the IM phenomenon in more depth:

- *Learn how instant messaging works.* Visit your text support site at www.thomsonedu.com/bcomm/lehman to learn more about instant messaging. From the Chapter 1 Electronic Café, you can access an online article describing how instant messaging works. Be prepared to discuss in class the features and uses of IM or follow your instructor's directions about how to use this information.

- *Read about how instant messaging can be an advantage and disadvantage at work.* Access the Business & Company Resource Center at http://bcrc.swlearning.com or another database available from your campus library to read more about the use of instant messaging in the workplace. Locate the following full-text articles:

  Gurliacci, D. (2004, November 22). Instant messaging at work has drawbacks. *Fairfield County Business Journal,* p. 5.

  Montague, C. (2005, January 17). Companies grapple with the pros and cons of workplace instant messaging. *Akron Beacon Journal.*

  Compile a list of advantages and a list of disadvantages of using IM in the workplace.

- *Participate in an online chat.* Your instructor will give you directions about how and when to log on to your online course and participate in an online chat on the following topic: *Instant messaging can be an effective business tool if . . .*

- *Consider helpful tips for using instant messaging.* Access your text support site at www.thomsonedu.com/bcomm/lehman to find helpful tips on using instant messaging as a business communication tool.

7.4 your turn Career Portfolio

Consider a situation in your career field in which you will have to say no to a request from a client or customer. Compose a letter to a fictitious individual that conveys the "no" with tact and consideration. See Appendix A for appropriate letter format.

7.3 your turn You're the Professional

As payroll manager, you have received the names of company employees who will be laid off over the next two weeks due to downsizing. Stacy Simms, a member of the sales team, lives in your neighborhood and occasionally socializes with you and your spouse. She has emailed you to find out if she is on the layoff list, as she is considering buying a new home.

- What are the ethical issues involved in this situation?
- What will you tell Stacy?
- Would your answer be different, depending on whether or not she is on the layoff list?

Case Analysis

Cybertheft: It's a Big Deal

One of the World Wide Web's most attractive features, easy access to a universe of information and data, is also one of its greatest vulnerabilities. Computer users can easily access, download, copy, cut, paste, and publish any of the text, pictures, video, sound, program code, and other data forms available on the Internet. An inherent conflict of interest prevails because of the consumer's appetite for data and the creator's right to remuneration for original work.

Copyrights provide an economic incentive for the development of creative works in literature, computer applications, and the performing arts. For instance, songwriters in the United States are paid royalties by radio stations for broadcasting their copyrighted musical works. Because of copyrights, it is illegal to make and sell an unauthorized duplicate of a commercial CD, video, or DVD. The law assures that creators receive remuneration from sales for their investment of time, talent, and energy. The information superhighway, however, crosses borders where U.S. copyright laws do not apply. With proper equipment and the aid of file sharing websites, cyberfans can make high-quality digital copies of downloaded music and movies, effectively bypassing copyright requirements.

Passage of the Patriot Act gave the FBI easier access to information about cyberspace theft by allowing examination of Internet databases without search warrants. Internet service providers have been compelled to turn over the names of subscribers traced by the music industry to their IP addresses. The Recording Industry Association has also targeted college campuses in its aggressive campaign to curtail unauthorized music downloading. In 2003, for example, four students agreed to fines of $12,000 to $17,500 each and promised to stop illegally downloading music on their campus computer servers as part of an out-of-court settlement. Some universities are also denying Internet access to students who download films and music illegally.[11]

Web pages are another type of creative expression falling victim to cybertheft. Dealernet, an organization that helps car dealers sell vehicles over the Internet, was shocked to discover that a Southern California company had downloaded Dealernet web pages and reproduced them on its own website. The competing site deleted the pages when Dealernet threatened legal action.

Cybertheft deprives musicians, artists, and other creative parties from the income that would otherwise result from the

Legal & Ethical

Students will be called upon to make quick and ethical decisions both on the job and as they market themselves to prospective employees. Real-world cases in every chapter and in online videos give students extensive practice in developing and applying ethical decision-making skills.

Diversity

Because today's diverse workplace demands that business communicators speak effectively to a wide range of audiences, students need to be skilled in inclusive language and fully aware of the levels of meaning and interpretation. *Business Communication, 15e* helps students prepare for this challenge and engages students in practical application of communication strategies that are respectful of all cultures and individuals.

Inside View
Part 5

In today's diverse world, employers interview job candidates from various cultures. Cross-cultural interviewing can increase the chances for misunderstanding or rejecting a talented candidate. Handshakes, eye contact, body language, and dress are among the culturally related factors that may influence an interviewer's success. How can you avoid making a negative impression during a job interview? As an employer, how will you avoid making false assumptions during a cross-cultural interview? View the Part V "The Job Interview" video segment online at http://www.thomsonedu.com/bcomm/lehman to learn more about the problem of cultural barriers in job interviews.

This content and the video segment will go on the web "The Job Interview," Communication Scenarios, Volume III, Segment 3.

The Job Interview

All recruiters want to hire the best candidates, but cross-cultural misunderstandings during the interview may lead to rejection of qualified individuals. Candidates from different nationalities and cultures can be discriminated against through ... ceptions and poor judgments in cross-cultural interviews.

...ct:

...ow can an interviewer's assumptions about what should ...r should not happen in an interview create cultural ...disperceptions?

...hat elements of body language and physical appearance ...an cause cultural misunderstandings?

...ow can eye contact, tone of voice, posture, showing

React:

Locate the following article that provides suggestions on cross-cultural interviewing. Neil Payne, Managing Director of Kwintessential Ltd., discusses the difficulties managers can encounter when interviewing applicants of various cultures.

Payne, N. (2006). Cross cultural interviews. *MilitaryJobHunts Career News & Global Strategy Report*. Retrieved August 30, 2006, from www.militaryjobhunts.com/career_news_global_strategy_report/7865.php

- List several questions you should avoid when conducting a cross-cultural job interview. Consider how asking a Hispanic person "How good is your Spanish?" could possibly be offensive.

SHOWCASE PART 1

GE: Do You Have What It Takes?

Imagine, solve, build, and lead—four bold verbs that express what it is to be part of GE. Known for its demanding high-performance culture, GE also recognizes the value of work/life flexibility in helping employees feel fulfilled both professionally and personally. Made up of 11 technology, services, and financial businesses with more than 300,000 employees worldwide, GE heads the list of Top 20 Companies for Leaders and strives to create a balance between the value that employees contribute to the company and the rewards offered in return.[1]

At GE, good ideas and a strong work ethic are encouraged, with company values based on three traditions: unyielding integrity, commitment to performance, and thirst for change. GE seeks qualified applicants who are willing to learn the skills necessary for company success. Some candidates are hired directly into leadership development programs that combine work experience with education and training. The Risk Management Leadership Program develops risk management leaders in a combination of rotation in various risk management positions and education in state-of-the-art risk management techniques. The Global Leadership Development Program grooms international leaders through a combination of global assignments and management training.

Diversity isn't just a noble idea at GE but an ongoing initiative, evidenced by the fact that women make up 35 percent of entry-level full-time corporate training programs hires, and minorities make up about 30 percent.[2] In an atmosphere of inclusiveness, all employees are encouraged to contribute and succeed. Former CEO and business legend Jack Welch offers the following career advice to anyone looking for the right job: "Choose something you love to do, make sure you're with people you like, and then give it your all."[3] At GE, "bringing good things to life" begins with offering opportunities to those who have a vision and the energy and confidence to pursue it. Success for GE, as for every company, begins with hiring well. The interview process provides the prospective employer with the opportunity to observe your talents and abilities, as well as your people skills. The interview is also your opportunity to form an impression of the company, its culture, and your future supervisors and coworkers.

Choose something you love to do, make sure you're with people you like, and then give it your all.

http://www.ge.com

Five *Your Turn* opportunities in each chapter are interactive points for student involvement:

Miscue uses real-world examples of miscommunication to teach prevention strategies and effective communication.

You're the Professional puts students into business scenarios and asks them to make an ethical response and justify their actions.

Career Portfolio guides students through the creation of documents that showcase their skills and prepare them to compete in the job market.

Assessment lets students know if they have mastered and applied core communication skills.

Electronic Café connects the text to the web and provides practice with instant and text messaging, discussion boards, intranets, web pages and other technology-driven communication tools.

Stepping Forward with Assessment and Technology

Assessment Tools

Both within the text and the accompanying technology, the new edition of *Business Communication* works with instructors to drive assessment in the course. ThomsonNOW™ for *Business Communication, 15e* is designed specifically to align with current requirements from the AACSB, helping instructors to track students' progress and provide assurance of learning reports to accrediting bodies. Assessment is addressed with self-assessments found in each chapter, through a variety of end-of-chapter materials, and by helping students develop their own portfolios of work. With ThomsonNOW for *Business Communication, 15e*, instructors have many options for measuring students' mastery of concepts!

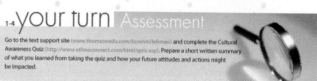

1-4 your turn Assessment

Go to the text support site (www.thomsonedu.com/bcomm/lehman) and complete the Cultural Awareness Quiz (http://www.ethnoconnect.com/html/quiz.asp). Prepare a short written summary of what you learned from taking the quiz and how your future attitudes and actions might be impacted.

8-2 your turn Assessment

Some career fields seem to have a bad public image. Lawyers, politicians, and reporters are often held in low esteem, but used car salespeople typically top the list of least trusted. They're often viewed as overly enthusiastic people who scream their way through annoying TV commercials. Even worse, they are often perceived as unscrupulous or even dishonest. Being trusted as an ethical person with good intentions is essential to effective persuasion. You can assess your own work ethics by completing the ethics quiz located at: http://encarta.msn.com/encnet/departments/elearning/?page=BizEthicsQuiz&Quizid=188&GT1=7004.

Email your instructor, explaining what you learned from the quiz and how ethical persuasion will be important in your career activities.

Text Web Site

http://lehman.swlearning.com
Lehman and DuFrene's password-protected web site is a robust teaching/learning center with innovative teaching suggestions for traditional classroom presentations and distance learning delivery, assessment guidelines, GMAT applications, supplementary case problems and much more.

Technology

ThomsonNOW™

The only web-based course management tool developed and tested by instructors to closely mirror each aspect of the teaching workflow, ThomsonNOW enhances student performance and saves instructors hours of time. It can be easily integrated into the instructor's course presentation or used by students without instructor involvement.

ThomsonNOW features the most intuitive, easiest-to-use interface on the market—a straightforward "tabbed" interface that allows navigation to all key functions with a single click. A unique home page tracks workflow. The program is inherently customizable—instructors can use one feature or all integrated aspects for more power, control, and efficiency.

Instructors can use ThomsonNOW to:
- **Plan** curriculum
- **Manage** the course and communicate with students
- **Teach** with more freedom
- **Assign** practice or homework to reinforce key concepts
- **Assess** student performance outcomes
- **Grade** with efficiency and control

Find out more at **www.thomsonedu.com/thomsonnow**.

Thomson NOW!

Just What You Need to Know and Do NOW!

ThomsonNOW is an online teaching and learning resource that gives you more control in less time and delivers the results you want—NOW!

What instructors are saying...

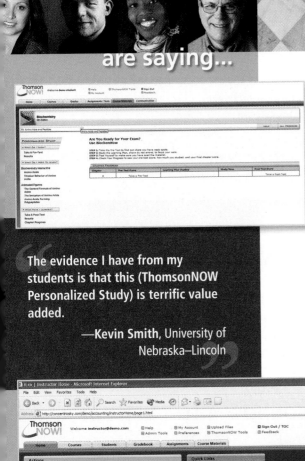

> The evidence I have from my students is that this (ThomsonNOW Personalized Study) is terrific value added.
>
> —**Kevin Smith**, University of Nebraska–Lincoln

> What I like most about ThomsonNOW is the simplicity of using it...
>
> —**Mina Yavari**, Hancock College

THOMSONNOW IS AN ONLINE TEACHING AND LEARNING RESOURCE.

ThomsonNOW offers all of your teaching and learning resources in one intuitive program organized around the essential activities you perform for class - lecturing, creating assignments, grading, quizzing, and tracking student progress and performance. ThomsonNOW's intuitive "tabbed" design allows you to navigate to all key functions with a single click and a unique homepage tell you just what needs to be done and when. ThomsonNOW, in most cases, provides students access to an integrated eBook, interactive tutorials, videos, animations, games, and other multimedia tools to help them get the most out of your course.

THOMSONNOW PROVIDES MORE CONTROL IN LESS TIME

ThomsonNOW's flexible assignment and grade book options provides you more control while saving you valuable time in planning and managing your course assignments. With ThomsonNOW, you can automatically grade all assignments, weigh grades, choose points or percentages and set the number of attempts and due dates per problem to best suit your overall course plan.

THOMSONNOW DELIVERS RESULTS

ThomsonNOW Personalized Study; a diagnostic tool (featuring a chapter specific Pre-test, Study Plan, and Post-test) empowers students to master concepts, prepare for exams, and be more involved in class. It's easy to assign and if you want, results will automatically post to your grade book. Results to Personalize Study provide immediate and ongoing feedback regarding what students are mastering and why they're not - to both you and the student. In most cases, Personalized Study links to an integrated eBook so students can easily review topics.

www.thomsonedu.com/ThomsonNOW

THOMSONNOW MAKES IT EASIER TO DO WHAT YOU ALREADY DO.

Designed by instructors for instructors, ThomsonNOW mirrors your natural workflow and provides time-saving, performance-enhancing tools for you and your students—**all in one program!**

YOU CAN USE THOMSONNOW TO...

- ▶ **Plan** your curriculum;
- ▶ **Manage** your course and communicate with students;
- ▶ **Teach** with more freedom;
- ▶ **Assign** practice or homework to reinforce key concepts;
- ▶ **Assess** student performance outcomes;
- ▶ **Grade** with efficiency and control to get the results you want.

STUDENTS CAN USE THOMSONNOW TO...

- ▶ **Manage** their time;
- ▶ **Prepare** for class;
- ▶ **Practice & Reinforce** key concepts learned in class;
- ▶ **Study** for exams more effectively;
- ▶ **Get the Grade** they want.

The flexibility of ThomsonNOW allows you to use a single aspect of the program, or for maximum power and effectiveness, to use all of the teaching and learning resources to create and customize your own material to match your course objectives.

THOMSONNOW SEAMLESSLY INTEGRATES WITH POPULAR COURSE MANAGEMENT PROGRAMS

ThomsonNOW on Blackboard, WebCT, eCollege, and Sakai provides students with seamless single sign-on access to ThomsonNOW through the school's course management system (CMS). After entering a simple access code just once at the beginning of the term, students get seamless access to both their CMS and ThomsonNOW textbook specific assignments and activities, with results flowing to your Blackboard, WebCT, eCollege, or Sakai gradebook. Rich content, seamless integration with ThomsonNOW functionality, and only one gradebook to manage.

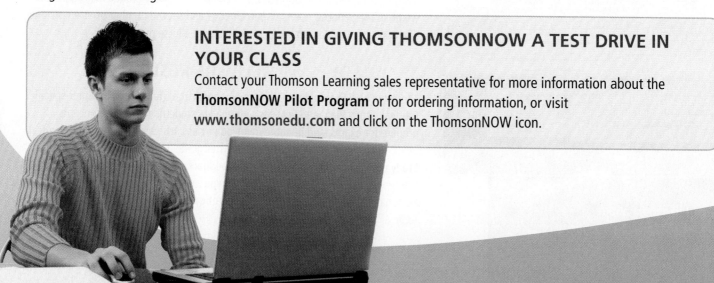

INTERESTED IN GIVING THOMSONNOW A TEST DRIVE IN YOUR CLASS

Contact your Thomson Learning sales representative for more information about the **ThomsonNOW Pilot Program** or for ordering information, or visit **www.thomsonedu.com** and click on the ThomsonNOW icon.

www.thomsonedu.com/ThomsonNOW

Business Communication

15e

Part 1 Communication Foundations

Establishing a Framework for Business Communication 1

Focusing on Interpersonal and Group Communication 2

Chapter 1
Establishing a Framework for Business Communication

Objectives

When you have completed Chapter 1, you will be able to:

1 Define communication and describe the main purpose for communication in business.

2 Explain the communication process model and the ultimate objective of the communication process.

3 Discuss how information flows in an organization (through various levels; formally and informally; and downward, upward, and horizontally).

4 Explain how legal and ethical constraints, diversity challenges, changing technology, and team environment act as strategic forces that influence the process of business communication.

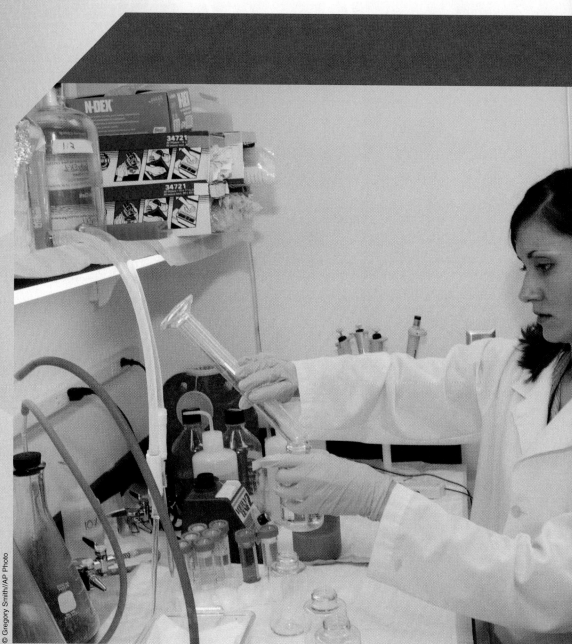

© Gregory Smith/AP Photo

Communication Challenges at the CDC

The events of September 11, 2001, affected every American citizen as well as the nation's business community. One agency whose mission was changed forever was the Centers for Disease Control and Prevention (CDC). The Atlanta-based federal agency, which is responsible for protecting Americans against infectious diseases and other health hazards, was instantly required to retool to meet the looming threat of bioterrorism, including anthrax, smallpox, and other deadly disease agents.

The CDC is one of 11 federal agencies under the Department of Health and Human Services. The agency stores and controls the nation's stockpile of smallpox vaccine and leads 3,000 local public health departments in devising a plan for containing an outbreak or epidemic and administering the vaccine. It must also meld its work with national security agencies, such as the CIA, the FBI, and the Department of Homeland Security.[1]

The leadership of the CDC must balance the urgent goal of preparing for a bioterrorism emergency with the agency's fundamental mission of preventing and controlling infectious disease and other health hazards. AIDS, cigarette smoking, obesity, Type II diabetes, and asthma are among the real, long-term problems that are equally crucial to public health. In addition, new threats, such as the West Nile virus and avian flu, regularly present themselves.

According to Julie Gerberding, director of the CDC, "ultimately, our customers are the citizens of the United States, so we have to have a better understanding of what they need to improve their health—what works and what doesn't work, from their perspective."[2] She describes her agency's key communication partners as the state and local health departments who monitor citizens' health, the people who run health plans and market preventive services, and the entire business community, which has a strong interest in promoting the health of its employees. She knows the importance of effective communication with a broad audience. Such a process identifies strengths and weaknesses in programs and helps make the CDC a more credible advocate when it asks for funding to address potential episodes of bioterrorism as well as chronic health problems unrelated to terrorism. To be effective in any work setting, you need to understand the process of communication and the dynamic environment in which it occurs.

> *Ultimately, our customers are the citizens of the United States, so we have to have a better understanding of what they need to improve their health—what works and what doesn't work, from their perspective."*

http://www.cdc.gov

SEE SHOWCASE, PART 2, ON PAGE 8, FOR SPOTLIGHT COMMUNICATOR JULIE GERBERDING, DIRECTOR OF THE CDC.

Purposes of Communication

Objective 1
Define communication and describe the main purpose for communication in business.

We communicate to satisfy needs in both our work and nonwork lives. Each of us wants to be heard, appreciated, and wanted. We also want to accomplish tasks and achieve goals. Obviously, then, a major purpose of communication is to help people feel good about themselves and about their friends, groups, and organizations. Generally people communicate for three basic purposes: to inform, to persuade, and to entertain.

What is communication? For our purposes, communication is the process of exchanging information and meaning between or among individuals through a common system of symbols, signs, and behavior. Other words used to describe the communication process include expressing feelings, conversing, speaking, corresponding, writing, listening, and exchanging. Studies indicate that managers typically spend 60 to 80 percent of their time involved in communication. In your career activities, you may communicate in a wide variety of ways, including

In what ways will communication be important in the career field you have chosen?

- attending meetings and writing reports related to strategic plans and company policy.
- presenting information to large and small groups.
- explaining and clarifying management procedures and work assignments.
- coordinating the work of various employees, departments, and other work groups.
- evaluating and counseling employees.
- promoting the company's products/services and image.

Whatever your chosen career field, communication skills will be an important requirement for you as a job applicant. Throughout this text, you will have the opportunity to develop and document your business communication skills through your Career Portfolio. This portfolio will provide evidence to you and future employers that you possess the essential knowledge and skills to be an effective communicator in today's workplace.

The Communication Process

Objective 2
Explain the communication process model and the ultimate objective of the communication process.

Effective business communication is essential to success in today's work environments. Recent surveys of executives document that abilities in writing and speaking are major determinants of career success in many fields.[3] Although essential to personal and professional success, effective business communication does not occur automatically. Your own experiences have likely taught you that a message is not interpreted correctly just because you transmitted it. An effective communicator anticipates possible breakdowns in the communication process— the unlimited ways the message can be misunderstood. This mind-set provides the concentration to design the initial message effectively and to be prepared to intervene at the appropriate time to ensure that the message received is on target—that is, as close as possible to what is intended.

Consider the communication process model presented in Figure 1-1. These seemingly simple steps actually represent a very complex process.

Figure 1-1 | **The Communication Process Model**

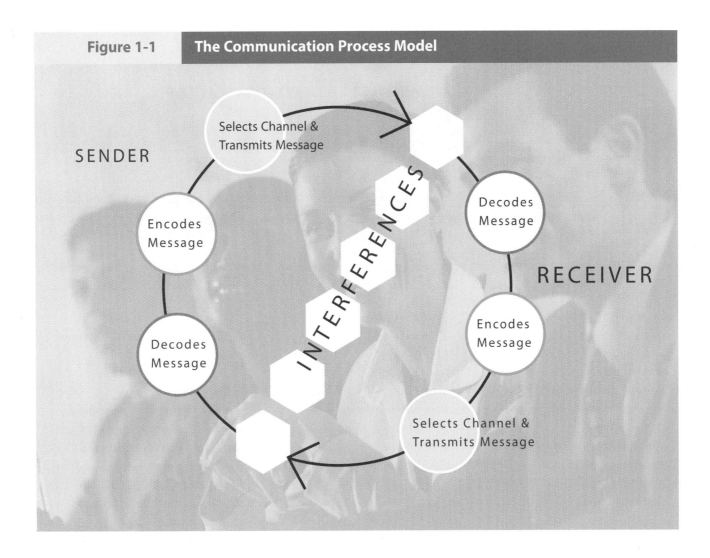

The Sender Encodes the Message

The sender carefully designs a message by selecting (1) words that clearly convey the message and (2) nonverbal signals (gestures, stance, tone of voice, and so on) that reinforce the verbal message. The process of selecting and organizing the message is referred to as **encoding**. The sender's primary objective is to encode the message in such a way that the message received is as close as possible to the message sent. Knowledge of the receiver's educational level, experience, viewpoints, and other information aids the sender in encoding the message. If information about the receiver is unavailable, the sender can put himself or herself in the receiver's position to gain fairly accurate insight for encoding the message. As you study Chapters 3 and 4, you will learn to use language effectively; Chapter 2 will assist you in refining your nonverbal communication.

Various behaviors can cause breakdowns in the communication process at the encoding stage, such as when the sender uses

What breakdowns in the encoding process have you experienced?

- words not present in the receiver's vocabulary.

- ambiguous, nonspecific ideas that distort the message.

- nonverbal signals that contradict the verbal message.

- expressions such as "uh" or grammatical errors, mannerisms (excessive hand movements, jingling keys), or dress styles that distract the receiver.

Figure 1-2 | **Channels of Communication**

TWO-WAY, FACE-TO-FACE

Examples: Informal conversations, interviews, oral presentations, speeches, and videoconferences
Advantages: Instant feedback, nonverbal signals, personal connection
Special considerations: Usually appropriate for conveying sensitive or unpleasant news

TWO-WAY, NOT FACE-TO-FACE

Examples: Telephone conversations, online chats
Advantages: Instant feedback, real-time connection
Special considerations: Lacks nonverbal elements, so verbal message must be especially clear

ONE-WAY, NOT FACE-TO-FACE

Examples: Letters, memos, reports, and electronic communications including email, fax, voice mail, and web page information
Advantages: Message considered more permanent and official
Special considerations: Lacks both nonverbal elements and instant feedback, so possible confusion must be anticipated and prevented

Which channel would be the most appropriate for communicating the following messages? Justify your answer.

- *Ask a client for additional information needed to provide requested services.*
- *Inform a customer that an order cannot be delivered on the date specified in the contract.*
- *Inform the sales staff of a special sales incentive (effective six weeks from now).*

The Sender Selects an Appropriate Channel and Transmits the Message

To increase the likelihood that the receiver will understand the message, the sender carefully selects an appropriate channel for transmitting the message. Three typical communication channels are illustrated in Figure 1-2.

Selecting an inappropriate channel can cause the message to be misunderstood and can adversely affect human relations with the receiver. For example, for a complex subject, a sender might begin with a written document and follow up with a face-to-face or telephone discussion after the receiver has had an opportunity to study the document. Written documents are required when legal matters are involved and written records must be retained.

The Receiver Decodes the Message

The receiver is the destination of the message. The receiver's task is to interpret the sender's message, both verbal and nonverbal, with as little distortion as possible. The process of interpreting the message is referred to as ***decoding***. Because words and

your turn MISCUE

The death of an 8-year-old school bus rider in Florida could have been prevented if the driver had received complete instructions about the child's drop-off point. As a dispatcher dictated route information, the substitute driver failed to note that the child should be dropped off on the west side of a specific intersection. The child was hit by traffic as she attempted to cross the intersection to the corner where she should have been dropped off.[4]

- Can you describe a similar communication misstep?
- What were the consequences?
- What steps could have been taken to have avoided this dilemma?

Give examples of nonverbal gestures that have different meanings among generations or cultures.

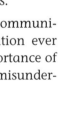

nonverbal signals have different meanings to different people, countless problems can occur at this point in the communication process:

- The sender inadequately encodes the original message with words not present in the receiver's vocabulary; ambiguous, nonspecific ideas; or nonverbal signals that distract the receiver or contradict the verbal message.

- The receiver is intimidated by the position or authority of the sender, resulting in tension that prevents the receiver from concentrating effectively on the message and failure to ask for needed clarification.

- The receiver prejudges the topic as too boring or difficult to understand and does not attempt to understand the message.

- The receiver is close-minded and unreceptive to new and different ideas.

The infinite number of breakdowns possible at each stage of the communication process makes us marvel that mutually satisfying communication ever occurs. The complexity of the communication process amplifies the importance of the next stage in the communication process—feedback to clarify misunderstandings.

The Receiver Encodes the Message to Clarify Any Misunderstandings

Both internal barriers and external barriers make communication challenging. How?

When the receiver responds to the sender's message, the response is called **feedback**. The feedback may prompt the sender to modify or adjust the original message to make it clearer to the receiver. Feedback may be verbal or nonverbal. A remark such as "Could you clarify . . ." or a perplexed facial expression provides clear feedback to the sender that the receiver does not yet understand the message. Conversely, a confident "Yes, I understand," and a nod of the head likely signal understanding or encouragement.

Chapter 1 • Establishing a Framework for Business Communication **7**

© Alex Wong/Meet The Press/Getty Images

Spotlight Communicator:
Julie Gerberding

DIRECTOR, CENTERS FOR DISEASE CONTROL

Leadership for the Times

Dr. Julie Gerberding is the first woman to lead the Centers for Disease Control and Prevention (CDC), the nation's premier public health agency, with more than 8,500 employees nationwide and a $6.8 billion budget. At the age of only 46, she was named director of the agency in 2002, arriving at a time of great opportunity and substantial challenge. The anthrax attacks brought heightened visibility as well as new responsibilities and resources.

Gerberding's background was uniquely suited to the new demands of a CDC director. A solid scientist, she had previously served for nearly two decades at the University of California, San Francisco, where she established herself as a leading expert in the treatment of AIDS. She was acting deputy director of the CDC's National Center for Infectious Diseases when the anthrax attacks began. It was during the mail-launched bioterrorist attack that Gerberding rose to national prominence as a top CDC spokeswoman, earning praise from politicians and public health groups for her straightforward style and expertise. "She is a very sensible, extraordinarily well-informed person who doesn't hide behind jargon or the idea that she has special knowledge about complicated matters that she really can't quite explain," said Dr. Julius R. Krevans, chancellor emeritus at UC San Francisco, who has known her since she was an intern.[5] Gerberding successfully combines professional talent as an infectious disease physician with exemplary leadership and exceptional communication skills.

When asked her opinion about some of the CDC tasks being given over to the Department of Homeland Security, Dr. Gerberding replied: "I'm not a territorial person. As a leader, I have found time

As a leader, I have found time and time again that if you step away from your turf issues and look at the general goal, very often you can gain by collaborating. Sometimes that means you give up a little now in order to gain more support than you started with."

and time again that if you step away from your turf issues and look at the general goal, very often you can gain by collaborating. Sometimes that means you give up a little now in order to gain more support than you started with." A firm believer in collaboration, Gerberding invites input from her staff and from medical community partners. Gerberding's solid academic background has resulted in a stronger relationship with the national health agencies, hospitals, and other medical deliverers who focus on the science, research, and treatment of diseases. She understands the importance of renowned scientists working with local health care providers to make sure the best information is communicated to the public.

Gerberding says that as frightening as it was, the anthrax crisis paved the way for more effective communication between the CDC and its constituents: "We had the attention of most Americans, many of whom may have been hearing for the first time what the CDC really is and does. We had the attention of Congress. We had a president come to the CDC for the first time in the history of the agency. If you take that kind of attention and appreciation for what our value is, and couple it with the investments in the public health system that are being made right now, it is an incredible opportunity."[6]

Applying What You Have Learned

1. What combination of communication skills is necessary for Julie Gerberding to be an effective director of the CDC?

2. How did Gerberding use adversity as a means to strengthen internal and external communication at the CDC?

3. Under what conditions is compromise appropriate? When is it not?

http://www.cdc.gov

SEE SHOWCASE, PART 3, ON PAGE 36, TO EXPAND YOUR KNOWLEDGE ABOUT COMMUNICATION AT THE CDC.

Interferences Hinder the Process

Consider a situation in which you have experienced a communication breakdown. What factors were responsible for the miscommunication? What could have been done to ensure successful communication?

Senders and receivers must learn to deal with the numerous factors that hinder the communication process. These factors are referred to as **interferences** or **barriers** to effective communication. Previous examples have illustrated some of the interferences that may occur at various stages of the communication process. For example,

- differences in educational level, experience, culture, and other characteristics of the sender and the receiver increase the complexity of encoding and decoding a message.
- physical interferences occurring in the channel include a noisy environment, interruptions, and uncomfortable surroundings.
- mental distractions, such as preoccupation with other matters and developing a response rather than listening.

You can surely compile a list of other barriers that affect your ability to communicate with friends, instructors, coworkers, supervisors, and others. By being aware of them, you can concentrate on removing these interferences.

Communicating Within Organizations

Objective 3
Discuss how information flows in an organization (through various levels; formally and informally; and downward, upward, and horizontally).

Organizational structure is the overall design of an organization, much like a blueprint developed to meet the company's specific needs and to enhance its ability to accomplish goals. A company's organizational structure is depicted graphically in an organization chart, as illustrated in Figure 1-3. An organizational chart helps define the scope of the organization and the division of specialized tasks among employees who work interdependently to accomplish common goals.

To be successful, organizations must create an environment that energizes and provides encouragement to employees to accomplish tasks by encouraging genuine openness and effective communication. **Organizational communication** is concerned with the movement of information within the company structure. Regardless of your career or level within an organization, your ability to communicate will affect not only the success of the organization but also your personal success and advancement within that organization.

Levels of Communication

Communication can involve sending messages to both large and small audiences. **Internal messages** are intended for recipients within the organization. **External messages** are directed to recipients outside the organization. When considering the intended audience, communication can be described as taking place on five levels, as shown in Figure 1-4, on page 11:

- **Intrapersonal communication**
- **Interpersonal communication**
- **Group communication**
- **Organizational communication**
- **Public communication**

Figure 1-3 | **Organization Chart of an Internet Company**

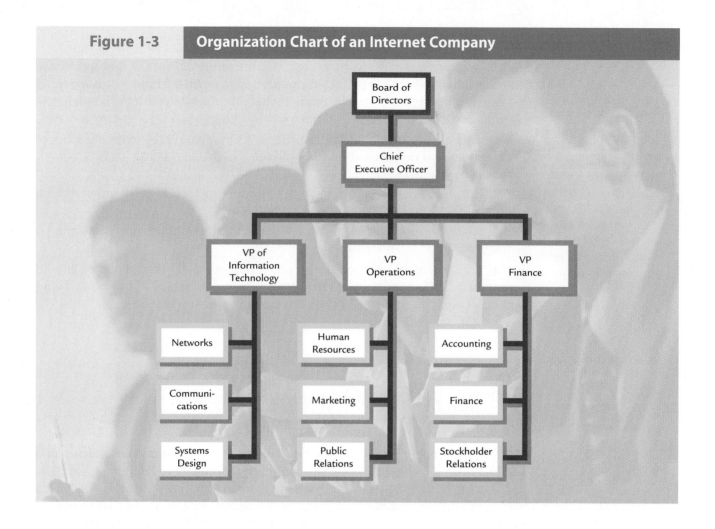

Communication Flow in Organizations

Communication occurs in a variety of ways in an organization. Some communication flows are planned and structured; others are not. Some communication flows can be formally depicted, whereas some defy description.

Formal and Informal Channels

The flow of communication within an organization follows both formal and informal channels.

- *Formal communication channel.* This channel is typified by the formal organization chart (see Figure 1-3), which is created by management to control individual and group behavior and to achieve the organization's goals. Essentially, the formal system is dictated by the technical, political, and economic environment of the organization. Within this system, people are required to behave in certain ways simply to get the work done.

- *Informal communication channel.* This channel develops as people interact within the formal, external system, and certain behavior patterns emerge—patterns that accommodate social and psychological needs. Because the informal channel undergoes continual changes, it cannot be depicted accurately by any graphic means.

Figure 1-4 | Levels of Communication

INTRAPERSONAL

- Communication within oneself
- Not considered by some to be true communication as it does not involve a separate sender and receiver

Examples: Individual reminding himself of tasks to complete or daily schedule

INTERPERSONAL

- Communication between two people
- Goals are to (1) accomplish the task confronting them (task goal), and (2) feel better about themselves and each other because of their interaction (maintenance goal)

Examples: Supervisor and subordinate, two coworkers

GROUP

- Communication among more than two people
- Goal of achieving greater output than individual efforts could produce

Examples: Committee or college class

ORGANIZATIONAL

- Groups combined in such a way that large tasks may be accomplished
- Goal of providing adequate structure for groups to achieve their purposes

Examples: Company or organization

PUBLIC

- The organization reaching out to its public to achieve its goals
- Goal of reaching many with the same message

Examples: Media advertisement, website communication

Why do organizations tend to become more bureaucratic as they grow in size?

When employees rely almost entirely on the formal communication system as a guide to behavior, the system might be identified as a *bureaucracy*. Procedures manuals, job descriptions, organization charts, and other written materials dictate the required behavior. Communication channels are followed strictly, and red tape is abundant. Procedures are generally followed exactly; terms such as *rules* and *policies* serve as sufficient reasons for actions. Even the most formal organizations, however, cannot function long before an informal communication system emerges. As people operate within the external system, they interact on a person-to-person basis and create an environment conducive to satisfying their personal emotions, prejudices, likes, and dislikes.

In the college classroom, for example, the student behavior required to satisfy the formal system is to attend class, take notes, read the text, and pass examinations. On the first day of class, this behavior is typical of almost all students, particularly if they did not know one another prior to attending the class. As the class progresses, however, the informal system emerges and overlaps the formal system. Students become acquainted, sit next to people they particularly like, talk informally, and may even plan ways to beat the external system. Cutting class and borrowing notes are examples. Soon, these behaviors become norms for class behavior. Students who do not engage in the informal system may be viewed with disdain by the others. Obviously, the informal system benefits people because it is efficient, and it affects the overall communication of the group in important ways.

The Grapevine as an Informal Communication System

Managers who ignore the grapevine have difficulty achieving organizational goals.

The **grapevine**, often called the *rumor mill*, is perhaps the best-known informal communication system. It is actually a component of the informal system. As people talk casually during coffee breaks and lunch periods, the focus usually shifts from topic to topic. One of the usual topics is work—job, company, supervisor, fellow employees. Even though the formal system has definite communication channels, the grapevine tends to develop and operate within all organizations. Consider these points concerning the accuracy and value of grapevine communication:

- As a communication channel, the grapevine has a reputation for being speedy but inaccurate. In the absence of alarms, the grapevine may be the most effective way to let occupants know that the building is on fire. It certainly beats sending a written memorandum or an email.

- Although the grapevine often is thought of as a channel for inaccurate communication, in reality, it is no more or less accurate than other channels. Even formal communication may become inaccurate as it passes from level to level in the organizational hierarchy.

Share a personal communication experience that involved the grapevine as an information source. How reliable was the message you sent or received? How time-efficient was the message transmission?

- The inaccuracy of the grapevine has more to do with the message input than with the output. For example, the grapevine is noted as a carrier of rumor, primarily because it carries informal messages. If the input is rumor, and nothing more, the output obviously will be inaccurate. But the output may be an accurate description of the original rumor.

- In a business office, news about promotions, personnel changes, company policy changes, and annual salary adjustments often is communicated by the grapevine long before being disseminated by formal channels. The process works similarly in colleges, where information about choice instructors typically is not published but is known by students from the grapevine. How best to prepare for

examinations, instructor attitudes on attendance and homework, and even future faculty personnel changes are messages that travel over the grapevine.

- A misconception about the grapevine is that the message passes from person to person until it finally reaches a person who can't pass it on—the end of the line. Actually, the grapevine works as a network channel. Typically, one person tells two or three others, who each tell two or three others, who each tell two or three others, and so on. Thus, the message may spread to a huge number of people in a short time.

- The grapevine has no single, consistent source. Messages may originate anywhere and follow various routes.

Due at least in part to widespread downsizing and corporate scandals during the last few years, employees in many organizations are demanding to be better informed. Some companies have implemented new formal ways for disseminating information to their internal constituents, such as newsletters and intranets. Company openness with employees, including financial information, means more information in the formal system rather than risking its miscommunication through informal channels. An employee of The Container Store—named the best company to work for in America—said that the company's willingness to divulge what it makes each year and its financial goals builds her trust in management.[7]

The Container Store

©//AP Graphics Bank

An informal communication system will emerge from even the most carefully designed formal system. Managers who ignore this fact are attempting to manage blindfolded. Instead of denying or condemning the grapevine, the effective manager will learn to *use* the informal communication network. The grapevine, for instance, can be useful in counteracting rumors and false information.

Directions for Communication Flow

The direction in which communication flows in an organization may be downward, upward, or horizontal, as shown in Figure 1-5. Because these three terms are used frequently in communication literature, they deserve clarification. Although the concept of flow seems simple, direction has meaning for those participating in the communication process.

Downward Communication. **Downward communication** flows from supervisor to employee, from policy makers to operating personnel, or from top to bottom on the organization chart. A simple policy statement from the top of the organization may grow into a formal plan for operation at lower levels. Teaching people how to perform their specific tasks is an element of downward communication. Another element is orientation to a company's rules, practices, procedures, history, and goals. Employees learn about the quality of their job performance through downward communication.

Downward communication normally involves both written and spoken methods and makes use of the following guidelines:

What would be an appropriate "rule of thumb" for a manager in deciding whether to send a written or spoken message to subordinates?

- People high in the organization usually have greater knowledge of the organization and its goals than do people at lower levels.

- Both spoken and written messages tend to become larger as they move downward through organizational levels. This expansion results from attempts to prevent distortion and is more noticeable in written messages.

- Spoken messages are subject to greater changes in meaning than are written messages.

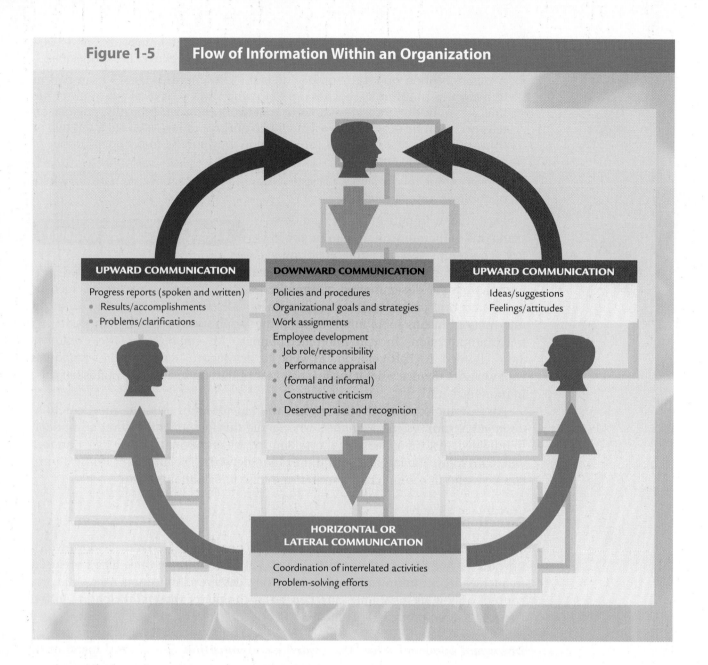

Figure 1-5 · Flow of Information Within an Organization

UPWARD COMMUNICATION

Progress reports (spoken and written)
- Results/accomplishments
- Problems/clarifications

DOWNWARD COMMUNICATION

Policies and procedures
Organizational goals and strategies
Work assignments
Employee development
- Job role/responsibility
- Performance appraisal
- (formal and informal)
- Constructive criticism
- Deserved praise and recognition

UPWARD COMMUNICATION

Ideas/suggestions
Feelings/attitudes

HORIZONTAL OR LATERAL COMMUNICATION

Coordination of interrelated activities
Problem-solving efforts

When a supervisor sends a message to a subordinate employee who then asks a question or nods assent, the question and the nod are signs of feedback. Feedback may flow both downward and upward in organizational communication.

What do you believe would be the typical communication patterns of a manager working under a win/lose philosophy? Under a win/win philosophy?

Upward Communication. Upward communication generally is feedback to downward communication. Although necessary and valuable, upward communication involves risks. When management requests information from lower organizational levels, the resulting information becomes feedback to that request. Employees talk to supervisors about themselves, their fellow employees, their work and methods of doing it, and their perceptions of the organization. These comments are feedback to the downward flow transmitted in both spoken and written form by

group meetings, procedures or operations manuals, company news releases, the company intranet, and the grapevine.

Accurate upward communication keeps management informed about the feelings of lower-level employees, taps the expertise of employees, helps management identify both difficult and potentially promotable employees, and paves the way for even more effective downward communication. Employees reporting upward are aware that their communications carry the risk of putting them on the spot or committing them to something they cannot handle.

Although employees typically appreciate and welcome genuine opportunities to send information to management, they will likely resent any superficial attempt to provide an open communication network with management. The following factors, then, are important to consider when upward communication flow is involved.

- Upward communication is primarily feedback to requests and actions of supervisors.

- Upward communication may be misleading because lower-level employees often tell the superior what they think the superior wants to hear. Therefore, their messages might contradict their true observations and perceptions.

- Upward communication is based on trust in the supervisor.

- Upward communication frequently involves risk to an employee.

- Employees will reject superficial attempts by management to obtain feedback from employees.

How can a manager maximize the effectiveness of horizontal communication among subordinates?

Horizontal Communication. Horizontal, or *lateral*, **communication** describes interactions between organizational units on the same hierarchical level. These interactions reveal one of the major shortcomings of organizational charts: They do not allow much room for horizontal communication when they depict authority relationships by placing one box higher than another and define role functions by placing titles in those boxes. Yet management should realize that horizontal communication is the primary means of achieving coordination in a functional organizational structure:

- Informal, horizontal communication takes place in any system or organization where people are available to one another. Horizontal communication serves a coordinating function in the organization. Units coordinate their activities to

accomplish task goals just as adjacent workers in a production line coordinate their activities.

- In an organization divided into cross-functional teams, horizontal communication among the team members is extremely important to achieve individual and team goals.

- Total Quality Management (TQM) experts emphasize that honest, open communication is the single most important factor in successfully creating a TQM environment. According to one TQM author, "if people keep talking to one another, they can work through their problems, overcome barriers, and find encouragement and support from others involved in quality efforts."[8]

A corporate study by the Ford Foundation found that productivity increased in companies that show concern for employees' personal lives and needs.

Many companies are realizing that the traditional hierarchy organized around functional units is inadequate for competing in increasingly competitive global markets. Companies utilize work teams that integrate work-flow processes rather than having specialists who deal with a single function or product. These cross-functional work teams break down the former communication barriers between isolated functional departments. Communication patterns take on varying forms to accommodate team activities.

Strategic Forces Influencing Business Communication

Objective 4
Explain how legal and ethical constraints, diversity challenges, changing technology, and team environment act as strategic forces that influence the process of business communication.

Communication is often a complicated process. Furthermore, communication does not take place in a vacuum, but rather is influenced by a number of forces at work in the environment. The effective communicator carefully considers each of these influences and structures communication responsively. Four critical forces influence the communication process and help to determine and define the nature of the communication that occurs, as shown in Figure 1-6.

Legal and Ethical Constraints as a Strategic Force Influencing Communication

How would you rank the four strategic forces in terms of magnitude of importance to business communication? Why?

Legal and ethical constraints act as a strategic force on communication in that they set boundaries in which communication can occur. International, federal, state, and local laws affect the way that various business activities can be conducted. For instance, laws specify that certain information must be stated in letters that reply to credit applications and those dealing with the collection of outstanding debts. Furthermore, one's own ethical standards will often influence what he or she is willing to say in a message. For example, a system of ethics built on honesty may require that the message provide full disclosure rather than a shrouding of the truth. Legal responsibilities, then, are the starting point for appropriate business communication. One's ethical belief system, or personal sense of right and wrong behavior, provides further boundaries for professional activity.

The press is full of examples of unethical conduct in the business community:

- Enron was found to have improved its financial image by moving debt off its books and using other

©//AP Graphics Bank

Figure 1-6 | **Strategic Forces Influencing Business Communication**

LEGAL & ETHICAL CONSTRAINTS

- International Laws
- Domestic Laws
- Code of Ethics
- Stakeholder Interests
- Ethical Frameworks
- Personal Values

CHANGING TECHNOLOGY

- Accuracy and Security Issues
- Telecommunications
- Software Applications
- "High-touch" Issues
- Telecommuting
- Databases

BUSINESS COMMUNICATION

DIVERSITY CHALLENGES

- Cultural Differences
- Language Barriers
- Gender Issues
- Education Levels
- Age Factors
- Nonverbal Differences

TEAM ENVIRONMENT

- Trust
- Team Roles
- Shared Goals and Expectations
- Synergy
- Group Reward
- Distributed Leadership

What recent events can you think of that have ethical themes?

accounting tricks. As a result of the scandal, thousands of company employees lost their jobs and their retirement investments while the company CEO made off with millions of dollars by selling Enron stock just before the company imploded.

- Accounting misrepresentations uncovered at WorldCom included the registering of a single sale many times over, thus inflating revenues by millions.

- Andersen Worldwide, a Big Five accounting giant and consulting service, suffered financial collapse following disclosures that it failed to report pervasive and blatant fraudulent practices among its client firms. "The name Andersen is likely to live on in the popular culture as Watergate did, a shorthand way to refer to scandal."[9]

- The United States is not the only country to experience recent lapses in ethical behavior among businesses. In Japan, for example, a recent scandal occurred at the company's largest utility, Tokyo Electric Power. Resignations of top officials followed revelations that the organization had issued falsified reports to nuclear safety regulators.[10]

Incidents such as these have far-reaching consequences. Those affected by decisions, the **stakeholders**, can include people inside and outside the organization. Employees and stockholders are obvious losers when a company fails. Competitors in the same industry also suffer, because their strategies are based on what they perceive about their competition. Beyond that, financial markets as a whole suffer due to erosion of public confidence. The recovery of the U.S. economy following the 2001 terrorist attack was further weakened because of the wounds from corporate scandals that resulted in severe drops in stock prices.

While laws represent statutory requirements for behavior, ethics are individually determined.

Business leaders, government officials, and citizens frequently express concern about the apparent erosion of ethical values in society. Even for those who want to do the right thing, matters of ethics are seldom clear-cut decisions of right versus wrong, and they often contain ambiguous elements. In addition, the pressure appears to be felt most strongly by lower-level managers, often recent business school graduates who are the least experienced at doing their jobs.

You can take steps now to prepare for dealing with pressure to compromise personal values:

- **Consider your personal value system.** Only if you have definite beliefs on a variety of issues and the courage to practice them will you be able to make sound ethical judgments. Putting ethical business practices first will also benefit your employing firm as its reputation for fairness and good judgment retains long-term clients or customers and brings in new ones.

- **Learn to analyze ethical dilemmas.** Knowing how to analyze ethical dilemmas and identify the consequences of your actions will help you make decisions that conform to your own value system. Thus, unless you know what you stand for and how to analyze ethical issues, you become a puppet, controlled by the motives of others, too weak to make a decision on your own.

The Foundation for Legal and Ethical Behavior

Although ethics is a common point of discussion, many find defining ethics challenging. Most people immediately associate ethics with standards and rules of conduct, morals, right and wrong, values, and honesty. Dr. Albert Schweitzer defined *ethics* as "the name we give to our concern for good behavior. We feel an obligation to consider not only our own personal well-being, but also that of others and of human society as a whole."[11] In other words, **ethics** refers to the principles of right and wrong that guide you in making decisions that consider the impact of your actions on others as well as yourself.

Although the recorded accounts of legal and ethical misconduct would seem to indicate that businesses are dishonest and unscrupulous, keep in mind that millions of business transactions are made daily on the basis of honesty and concern for the welfare of others. Why should a business make ethical decisions? What difference will it make? James E. Perrella, executive vice president of Ingersoll-Rand Company, gave a powerful reply to these questions:[12]

Our question of today should be, what's the right thing to do, the right way to behave, the right way to conduct business? Don't just ask, is it legal? Have you ever considered what business would be like if we all did it? If every businessman and businesswoman followed the Golden Rule? Many people, including many business leaders, would argue that such an application of ethics to business would adversely affect bottom-line performance. I say nay . . . . Good ethics, simply, is good business. Good ethics will attract investors. Good ethics will attract good employees. You can do what's right. Not because of conduct codes. Not because of rules or laws. But because you know what's right.

Identifying ethical issues in typical workplace situations may be difficult, and coworkers and superiors may apply pressure for seemingly logical reasons. To illustrate, examine each of the following workplace situations for a possible ethical dilemma:

What situations have you faced as a worker or student that caused ethical dilemmas?

- Corporate officers deliberately withhold information concerning a planned sellout to prevent an adverse effect on stock prices.

- A salesperson, who travels extensively, overstates car mileage to cover the cost of personal telephone calls that the company refuses to reimburse.

- To protect his job, a product engineer decides not to question a design flaw in a product that could lead to possible injuries and even deaths to consumers because the redesign would cause a delay in product introduction.

- To stay within the departmental budget, a supervisor authorizes a software program to be installed on 50 office computers when only one legal copy was purchased.

- Angry at a superior for an unfavorable performance appraisal, an employee leaks confidential information (e.g., trade secrets such as a recipe or product design, marketing strategies, or product development plans) to an acquaintance who works for a competitor.

Your fundamental morals and values provide the foundation for making ethical decisions. However, as the previous examples imply, even minor concessions in day-to-day decisions can gradually weaken an individual's ethical foundation.

Causes of Illegal and Unethical Behavior

Understanding the major causes of illegal and unethical behavior in the workplace will help you become sensitive to signals of escalating pressure to compromise your values. Unethical corporate behavior can have a number of causes:

- ***Excessive emphasis on profits.*** Business managers are often judged and paid on their ability to increase business profits. This emphasis on profits may send a message that the end justifies the means. According to former Federal Reserve Chairman Alan Greenspan, "infectious greed" ultimately pushed companies such as Enron, Global Crossing, and WorldCom into bankruptcy.[13]

- ***Misplaced corporate loyalty.*** A misplaced sense of corporate loyalty may cause an employee to do what seems to be in the best interest of the company, even if the act is illegal or unethical.

- ***Obsession with personal advancement.*** Employees who wish to outperform their peers or are working for the next promotion may feel that they cannot afford to fail. They may do whatever it takes to achieve the objectives assigned to them.

Figure 1-7

Four Dimensions of Business Behavior

DIMENSION 1 Behavior that is illegal and unethical	**DIMENSION 2** Behavior that is illegal, yet ethical
DIMENSION 3 Behavior that is legal, yet unethical	**DIMENSION 4** Behavior that is both legal and ethical

- **Expectation of not getting caught.** Employees who believe that the end justifies the means often believe that the illegal or unethical activity will never be discovered. Unfortunately, a great deal of improper behavior escapes detection in the business world. Believing no one will ever find out, employees are tempted to lie, steal, and perform other illegal acts.

"The speed of the leader is the speed of the pack" illustrates the importance of leading by example.

- **Unethical tone set by top management.** If top managers are not perceived as highly ethical, lower-level managers may be less ethical as a result. Employees have little incentive to act legally and ethically if their superiors do not set an example and encourage and reward such behavior. "The speed of the leader is the speed of the pack" illustrates the importance of leading by example.

- **Uncertainty about whether an action is wrong.** Many times, company personnel are placed in situations in which the line between right and wrong is not clearly defined. When caught in this gray area, the perplexed employee asks, "How far is too far?"

- **Unwillingness to take a stand for what is right.** Often employees know what is right or wrong but are not willing to take the risk of challenging a wrong action. They may lack the confidence or skill needed to confront others with sensitive legal or ethical issues. They may remain silent and then justify their unwillingness to act.

Framework for Analyzing Ethical Dilemmas

Determining whether an action is ethical can be difficult. Learning to analyze a dilemma from both legal and ethical perspectives will help you find a solution that conforms to your own personal values. Figure 1-7 shows the four conclusions you might reach when considering the advisability of a particular behavior.

How can you keep up with the legal requirements in your field?

Dimension 1: Behavior that is illegal and unethical. When considering some actions, you will reach the conclusion that they are both illegal and unethical. The law specifically outlines the "black" area—those alternatives that are clearly wrong, and your employer will expect you to become an expert in the laws that affect your particular area. When you encounter an unfamiliar area, you must investigate any possible legal implications. Obviously, obeying the law is in the best interest of all concerned: you as an individual, your company, and society. In addition, contractual agreements between the organization and another group provide explicit guidance in selecting an ethically responsible alternative. Frequently, your own individual sense of right and wrong will also confirm that the illegal action is wrong for you personally. In such situations, decisions about appropriate behavior are obvious.

Dimension 2: Behavior that is illegal, yet ethical. Occasionally, a businessperson may decide that even though a specific action is illegal, there is a justifiable reason to break the law. A case in point is a recent law passed in Vermont that makes it illegal for a pharmaceutical company to give any gift valued at $25 or more to doctors or their personnel.[14] Those supporting the law charge that the giving of freebies drives up medical costs by encouraging doctors to prescribe new, more expensive brand-name drugs. The law's opponents contend that the gifts do not influence doctors and are merely educational tools for new products. Although a pharmaceutical firm and its employees may see nothing wrong with providing gifts worth in excess of $25, they would be well advised to consider the penalty of $10,000 per violation before acting on their personal ethics. A more advised course of action probably would be to act within the law while lobbying for a change in the law.

Dimension 3: Behavior that is legal, yet unethical. If you determine that a behavior is legal and complies with relevant contractual agreements and company policy, your next step is to consult your company's or profession's **code of ethics**. This written document summarizes the company's or profession's standards of ethical conduct. Some companies refer to this document as a *credo* or *standards of ethical conduct*. If the behavior does not violate the code of ethics, then put it to the test of your own personal integrity. You may at times reject a legal action because it does not "feel right." Most Americans were appalled to learn that many leading figures in recent corporate scandals were never convicted of a single crime. Although they may have acted legally, their profiting at the expense of company employees, stockholders, and the public hardly seemed ethical. You may be faced with situations in which you reject a behavior that is legal because you would not be proud of your family and community knowing that you engaged in it.

Which of the ethical frameworks do you find most appropriate for you personally? Why?

Dimension 4: Behavior that is both legal and ethical. Decisions in this dimension are easy to make. Such actions comply with the law, company policies, and your professional and personal codes of ethics.

The Pagano Model offers a straightforward method for determining whether a proposed action is advisable.[15] For this system to work, you must answer the following six questions honestly:

- Is the proposed action legal—the core starting point?
- What are the benefits and costs to the people involved?
- Would you want this action to be a universal standard, appropriate for everyone?
- Does the action pass the light-of-day test? That is, if your action appeared on television or others learned about it, would you be proud?
- Does the action pass the Golden Rule test? That is, would you want the same to happen to you?
- Does the action pass the ventilation test? Ask the opinion of a wise friend with no investment in the outcome. Does this friend believe the action is ethical?

Martha Stewart was found guilty of conspiracy, obstruction of justice, and making false statements regarding her sale of shares of ImClone stock just before the company's downturn. Some have defended her

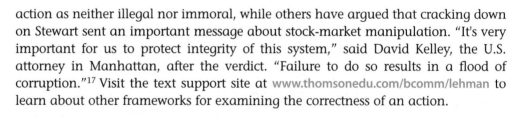

A senior executive in your company is running for the presidency of a professional organization. While assisting her in preparing a speech she will give to members of the organization, you read through the biographical information she provided to them. You note that some of the information does not match information in your company's files, as she seems to have claimed a fictitious degree and inflated other credentials. She tells you "It's nothing to worry about" when you meet with her and point out the discrepancies.[16] What do you do now?

A. Take her advice and not worry about it.

B. Contact the organization directly to correct the information without telling her about it.

C. Confront her, telling her you will have to report the incident if she does not correct the situation.

D. Bring the matter to the attention of senior management without saying anything more to the executive.

Describe the reasoning behind your chosen action.

action as neither illegal nor immoral, while others have argued that cracking down on Stewart sent an important message about stock-market manipulation. "It's very important for us to protect integrity of this system," said David Kelley, the U.S. attorney in Manhattan, after the verdict. "Failure to do so results in a flood of corruption."[17] Visit the text support site at www.thomsonedu.com/bcomm/lehman to learn about other frameworks for examining the correctness of an action.

Diversity Challenges as a Strategic Force Influencing Communication

Diversity in the workplace is another strategic force influencing communication. Differences between the sender and the receiver in areas such as culture, age, gender, and education require a sensitivity on the part of both parties so that the intended message is the one that is received.

Understanding how to communicate effectively with people from other cultures has become more integral to the work environment as many U.S. companies are increasingly conducting business with international companies or becoming multinational. Successful communication must often span barriers of language and requires a person to consider differing world views resulting from societal, religious, or other cultural factors. When a person fails to consider these factors, communication suffers, and the result is often embarrassing and potentially costly.

McDonald's is an example of a large U.S. company that has expanded its operations to include most major countries in the world. To be successful on an international scale, managers had to be aware of

cultural differences and be willing to work to ensure that effective communication occurred despite these barriers.

What is the relationship between political barriers and communication barriers?

Occasionally, however, a whopper of an intercultural communication faux pas occurs. That is what happened when McDonald's began its promotional campaign in Great Britain for the World Cup soccer championship. It seemed like a clever (and harmless) idea to reproduce the flags of the 24 nations participating in the event and print them on packaging—two million Happy Meal bags, to be exact. What marketing personnel failed to consider was that words from the *Koran* are printed on the Saudi flag. The idea that sacred words from Islam's holy book were mass printed to sell a product with the knowledge that the packages would be thrown into the trash angered and offended many Muslims, who immediately complained. McDonald's apologized for the gaffe and agreed to cooperate with the Saudis in finding a solution to the problem.[18]

While NAFTA has created new business opportunities for U.S. and Mexican entities, unique problems have also occurred. After seven trips to Mexico and nine months of courtship, a U.S. firm faxed the final contract to the Mexican CEO. This was a big mistake, because Mexican protocol calls for more formal finalizing in a face-to-face meeting.[19]

These errors serve as examples of how much "homework" is involved in maintaining good relations with customers or clients from other cultures. The potential barrier of language is obvious; however, successful managers know that much more is involved in communicating with everyone—across cultures, genders, ages, abilities, and other differences.

Communication Opportunities and Challenges in Diversity

As world markets expand, U.S. employees at home and abroad will be doing business with more people from other countries. You may find yourself working abroad for a large American company, an international company with a plant in the United States, or a company with an ethnically diverse workforce. Regardless of the workplace, your **diversity skills**, that is, your ability to communicate effectively with both men and women of all ages and with people of other cultures or minority groups, will affect your success in today's culturally diverse, global economy.

- **International issues.** Worldwide telecommunications and intense international business competition have fueled the movement of many industries into world markets. During the past four decades, U.S. firms have established facilities in Europe, Central and South America, and Asia. At many U.S. corporations, such as Dow Chemical, Gillette, and IBM, more than 40 percent of total sales in recent years has come from international operations. Over the past decade, Asians and Europeans have built plants in the United States. Many U.S. workers are now employed in manufacturing plants and facilities owned and operated by foreign interests. Understanding a person of another culture who may not speak your language well or understand your culturally based behaviors is a daily challenge faced by many. Specific guidelines for writing and speaking with an international audience are provided in later chapters.

How has diversity impacted the development of the United States as a world leader?

- **Intercultural issues.** Changing demographics in the United States are requiring businesses to face ethnic diversity in the workplace. Rather than being a melting pot for people from many countries, the United States offers an environment in which people of varying cultures can live and practice their cultural

Courtesy of International Business Machines Corporation. Unauthorized use not permitted.

heritage. People with a common heritage often form their own neighborhoods and work at retaining their traditional customs and language, while still sharing in the common culture. Consequently, *mosaic* seems to be a more accurate term

Figure 1-8 | **Changing Workforce Age Demographics**

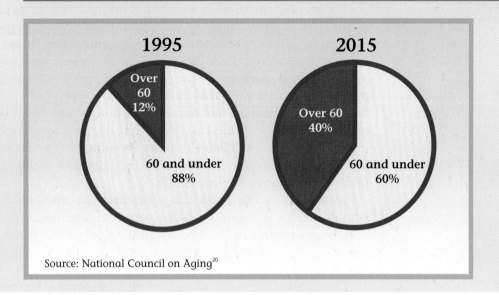

1995   2015

Over 60 12%

60 and under 88%

Over 60 40%

60 and under 60%

Source: National Council on Aging[20]

than *melting pot* to reflect U.S. cultural diversity. As in a mosaic, small, distinct groups combine to form the pattern or design of the U.S. population and workforce. U.S. labor statistics reflect the declining proportion of white males in the labor force and growing proportions of minorities and women.[21] People from different backgrounds invariably bring different values, attitudes, and perceptions to the workplace.

The "graying of America" reflects the growing numbers of people who are remaining in the workforce to an older and older age.

- **Intergenerational issues.** While age diversity has always been present in the workplace, recent trends have made it a more important issue than ever. The so-called "graying of America" has changed the age distribution in the U.S. population. The older segment of the population is larger today than at any time previously. The maturing of the "baby boomer" generation (those born between 1946 and 1964), a relatively low birthrate, and increasing life spans have led to a higher average age in the population. Today's workforce reflects the advancing age of the general populace. As of the year 2005, for instance, 40 percent of the workforce was 40 or older.[22] Figure 1-8 illustrates the continued trend toward an older workforce. Because of changes in laws affecting retirement benefits and better overall health, many older workers will choose to continue longer in their professional activities than in past years. Because of the broadening of the age span in the workplace, businesses will be faced with new challenges related to differences in perceptions, values, and communication styles of the generations. Chapter 3 includes a Strategic Forces focus on generational differences and their impact on workplace communication.

- **Gender issues.** The flood of women entering the job market has substantially changed the American workforce. Old social patterns of behavior that defined the appropriate roles for men and women do not fit in a work environment free from discrimination. Civil rights laws prohibiting sex discrimination and pay equity requirements have been in place for more than 30 years, yet charges continue to be filed by individuals who feel that their rights have been violated. The number of sexual harassment cases has increased in recent years, resulting from a broader-based definition of what constitutes sexual harassment. Although a charge of sexual harassment may be based on actions with sexual overtones, the offense has also been interpreted to include comments, visual images, or other conditions that create a hostile working environment. One result of the increased focus on sexual harassment in the workplace is the reluctance of some to communicate with other workers for fear that their actions or words might be misconstrued. Both men and women confront workplace communication challenges.

What other aspects of diversity can influence communication?

Workplace diversity can lead to misunderstandings and miscommunications, but it also poses opportunities to improve both workers and organizations. Managers must be prepared to communicate effectively with workers of different nationalities, genders, races, ages, abilities, and so forth.

Managing a diverse workforce effectively will require you to communicate with *everyone* and to help all employees reach their fullest potential and contribute to the company's goals. When miscommunication occurs, both sides are frustrated and often angry. To avoid such problems, increasing numbers of companies have undertaken **diversity initiatives** and are providing diversity-training seminars to help workers understand and appreciate gender and age differences and the cultures of coworkers. To prepare for these communication challenges, commit the time and energy to enhance your diversity skills while you are attending classes as well as after you enter the workplace.

Culture and Communication

What are some examples in your own community of culture-oriented activities?

Managers with the *desire* and the *skill* to conduct business in new international markets and to manage a diverse workforce effectively will confront problems created by cultural differences. The way messages are decoded and encoded is not just a function of the experiences, beliefs, and assumptions of the person sending or receiving those messages but also are shaped by the society in which he or she lives.

© William Howard/Stone/Getty Images

People learn patterns of behavior from their **culture**. The *culture* of a people is the product of their living experiences within their own society. Culture could be described as "the way of life" of a people and includes a vast array of behaviors and beliefs. These patterns affect how people perceive the world, what they value, and how they act. Differing patterns can also create barriers to communication. Visit the text support site at www.thomsonedu.com/bcomm/lehman to learn more about the characteristics of culture that shape communication.

Barriers to Intercultural Communication

Give several examples of stereotypes that prevail concerning certain cultural groups.

Because cultures give different definitions to such basics of interaction as values and norms, people raised in two different cultures may clash in various ways.

- **Ethnocentrism.** Problems occur between people of different cultures primarily because people tend to assume that their own cultural norms are the right way to do things. They wrongly believe that the specific patterns of behavior desired in their own cultures are universally valued. This belief, known as **enthnocentrism**, is certainly natural; but learning about other cultures and developing sensitivity will help minimize ethnocentric reactions when dealing with other cultures.

- **Stereotypes.** We often form a mental picture of the main characteristics of another group, creating preformed ideas of what people in this group are like. These pictures, called **stereotypes**, influence the way we interact with members of the other group. When we observe a behavior that conforms to the stereotype, the validity of the preconceived notion is reinforced. We often view the other person as a representative of a class of people rather than as an individual. People of all cultures have stereotypes about other cultural groups they have

Go to the text support site (www.thomsonedu.com/bcomm/lehman) and complete the Cultural Awareness Quiz (http://www.ethnoconnect.com/html/quiz.asp). Prepare a short written summary of what you learned from taking the quiz and how your future attitudes and actions might be impacted.

encountered. These stereotypes can interfere with communication when people interact on the basis of the imagined representative and not the real individual.

- **Interpretation of time.** The study of how a culture perceives time and its use is called **chronemics**. In the United States, we have a saying that "time is money." Canadians, like some northern Europeans who are also concerned about punctuality, make appointments, keep them, and do not waste time completing them. In some other cultures, time is the cheapest commodity and an inexhaustible resource; time represents a person's span on earth, which is only part of eternity. To these cultures, long casual conversations prior to serious discussions or negotiations is time well spent in establishing and nurturing relationships. On the other hand, the time-efficient American businessperson is likely to fret about the waste of precious time.

- **Personal space requirements.** Space operates as a language just as time does. The study of cultural space requirements is known as **proxemics**. In all cultures, the distance between people functions in communication as "personal space" or "personal territory." In the United States, for example, for intimate conversations with close friends and relatives, individuals are willing to stay within about a foot and a half of each other; for casual conversations, up to two or three feet; for job interviews and personal business, four to twelve feet; and for public occasions, more than twelve feet. However, in many cultures outside the United States, closer personal contact is accepted, or greater distance may be the norm.

Do differences exist in the nonverbal communication of people of different generations? Justify your answer.

- **Body language.** The study of body language is known as **kinesics**. Body language is not universal, but instead is learned from one's culture. Even the most basic gestures have varying cultural meanings—the familiar North American symbol for "okay" means zero in France, money in Japan, and an expression of vulgarity in Brazil. Similarly, eye contact, posture, and facial expressions carry different meanings throughout the world. Chapter 2 contains an expanded discussion of nonverbal communication.

Give some examples of words and phrases that have different meanings for speakers of British English than for speakers of American English.

- **Translation limitations.** Words in one language do not always have an equivalent meaning in other languages, and the concepts the words describe are often different as well. Translators can be helpful, but keep in mind that a translator is working with a second language and must listen to one language, mentally cast the words into another language, and then speak them. This process is difficult and opens the possibility that the translator will fall victim to one or more cultural barriers. The Case Analysis following Chapter 3 provides additional opportunity for you to explore translation issues.

Select a word with various synonyms. How are the meanings of each word somewhat different?

- **Lack of language training.** The following is an anecdote that speaks to the need for language training:

What do you call someone who speaks two languages? (Reply: bilingual)

What do you call someone who speaks three languages? (Reply: trilingual)

What do you call someone who speaks one language? (Reply: an American)

This tongue-in-cheek humor reinforces the language illiteracy of most U.S. citizens. Since familiarity with a second language improves your competitiveness as a job applicant, be sure to exploit that ability in your résumé. In some situations, learning a second language may not be feasible—you are completing a short-term assignment, you must leave immediately, or the language is extremely difficult to learn. Learning Japanese, for instance, involves understanding grammar, pronunciation, the writing system, and acquiring adequate vocabulary. While the sound system is simple to master compared with those of other languages, the challenging writing system requires learning 1,945 kanji characters. Everyday language use requires learning 1,945 kanji characters.[23]

Even if you cannot speak or write another language fluently, people from other cultures will appreciate simple efforts to learn a few common phrases. Other suggestions for overcoming language differences are discussed in the accompanying Strategic Forces feature, "Viva la Difference!"

Changing Technology as a Strategic Force Influencing Communication

Electronic tools have not eliminated the need for basic communication skills; they can, in fact, create new obstacles or barriers to communication that must be overcome. These tools, however, also create opportunities, which range from the kinds of communications that are possible to the quality of the messages themselves. Electronic tools, as shown in Figure 1-9 on page 29, can help people in various ways, such as (1) collecting and analyzing data, (2) shaping messages to be clearer and more effective, and (3) communicating quickly and efficiently with others over long distances.

In your opinion, what communication technology has most changed the way business is conducted?

Using various communication technologies, individuals can often work in their homes and send and receive work from the office electronically. **Telecommuting** offers various advantages, including reduced travel time and increased work flexibility. Laptops and PDAs provide computing power for professionals wherever they may be—in cars, hotel rooms, airports, or clients' offices.

The ability to find information quickly and easily is essential to organizational and personal success. Whereas the public Internet is accessible to everyone and offers a wide array of information, private databases provide specialized and advanced information on specific topics. Databases enable decision makers to obtain information quickly and accurately and offer these advantages:

- **Data organization**—the ability to organize large amounts of data.

In what way has word processing software become increasingly like desktop publishing software?

- **Data integrity**—assurance that the data will be accurate and complete.

- **Data security**—assurance that the data are secure because access to a database is controlled through several built-in data security features.

Internal databases contain proprietary information that is pertinent to the particular business or organization and its employees. External databases (networks) allow users to access information from remote locations literally around the world and in an instant transfer that information to their own computers for further manipulation or storage. Information is available on general news, stocks, financial markets, sports, travel, weather, and a variety of publications.

DIVERSITY CHALLENGES

Viva la Difference!

With so many barriers, communicating with people of other cultures can be difficult. Anyone who enters the business world today must be aware of potential trouble spots and of ways to avoid them. Application of some common sense guidelines can help to overcome intercultural barriers.

- **Learn about that person's culture.**

Many sources of useful information are available. University courses in international business communication are increasing, and experienced businesspeople have written books recounting some of the subtle but important ways that people from other cultures communicate.[24] Various Internet sites are dedicated to sharing information to help the intercultural communicator. Networking can generate the names of other businesspeople who have made successful contact with another culture. A telephone conversation or a lunch meeting may provide useful pointers on proper and improper behavior. Corporations with frequent and extensive dealings in other countries often establish workshops in which employees receive briefing and training before accepting overseas assignments. Learning the language is an invaluable way of becoming more familiar with another culture.

- **Have patience—with yourself and the other person.**

Conversing with someone from another culture, when one of you is likely to be unfamiliar with the language being used, can be difficult and time consuming. By being patient with mistakes, making sure that all questions are

© DCA Productions/Taxi/Getty Images

answered, and not hurrying, you are more likely to make the outcome of the conversation positive. You must also learn to be patient and tolerant of ambiguity. Being able to react to new, different, and unpredictable situations with little visible discomfort or irritation will prove invaluable. The author Howard Schuman writes that "a sense of humor is indispensable for dealing with the cultural mistakes and faux pas you will certainly commit."[25]

- **Get help when you need it.**

If you are not sure what is being said—or why something is being said in a certain way—ask for clarification. If you feel uneasy about conversing with someone from another culture, bring along someone you trust who understands that culture. You will have a resource if you need help.

Instead of ignoring cultural factors, workers and employers can improve communication by recognizing them and by considering people as individuals rather than as members of stereotypical groups. Many companies view the implementation of a diversity initiative as a way to improve organizational communication. The goal of such a program is to increase awareness and appreciation for areas of differences among employees and to build stronger rapport by finding commonalities. Firms with successful diversity initiatives find that promoting common understanding among workers boosts morale, creativity, and productivity.

Application

Interview a person from a cultural group other than your own. Include the following questions:

1. **What examples can you give of times when you experienced discrimination or isolation?**

2. **What information can you provide to aid other groups in understanding your cultural uniqueness?**

3. **What advice would you give for improving intercultural understanding?**

Figure 1-9 **Communication Technology Tools**

TOOLS FOR DATA COLLECTION AND ANALYSIS

Knowing how to collect information from the Internet and communicate in a networked world is critical. Generally, electronic communication provides researchers with two distinct advantages:

- Electronic searches can be done in a fraction of the time required to conduct manual searches of printed sources.
- The vast amount of information available allows researchers to develop better solutions to problems.

INTERNET

The vast "network of networks" links computers throughout the world. Information in the form of text, images, audio, and video is quickly available and easily searchable.

INTRANETS

Password-protected resources available via the Internet allow companies to post information and resources for employees.

EXTRANETS

Protected information and resources on company site are made available to customers, partners, or others with need to know.

TOOLS FOR SHAPING MESSAGES TO BE CLEARER AND MORE EFFECTIVE

Documents that took days to produce during the b.c. (before computers) era can now be created in hours and with a wide array of creative elements.

DOCUMENT PRODUCTION SOFTWARE

- Production of documents is expedited by ability to save, retrieve, and edit.
- Quality of messages is improved through spell check, thesaurus, writing analysis software, and print features.

ELECTRONIC PRESENTATIONS

- Multimedia presentations can include visuals that combine text, images, animation, sound, and video.
- Quality royalty-free multimedia content is available from third-party sources.

WEB PUBLISHING TOOLS

- Pages can be created without need for extensive knowledge of hypertext markup language, or HTML.
- Hyperlinks to other documents and websites can be included in the design.

COLLABORATIVE SOFTWARE

- Groups can write collaboratively, with each author marking revisions and inserting document comments for distribution to all coauthors.
- Some collaborative software programs allow

(continued on next page)

- Reports preparation is simplified by automatic generation of contents page, indexes, and documentation references.
- Mail merge feature allows for personalization of form letters. Typography and design elements can be used to create persuasive, professional communications.

- Images can be scanned or captured with digital cameras and recorders or generated using specialized software.
- Interactive whiteboards give speakers direct control over computer applications from the board, facilitate interaction using electronic ink to annotate visuals or record brainstorming ideas, and record annotated files for electronic distribution or later use.

- Formatted web pages may be viewed using a variety of web browsers.
- **Weblogs** (blogs) are websites that are updated on a frequent basis with new information about a particular subject(s). Information can be written by the site owner, gleaned from other websites or other sources, or contributed by users.

multiple authors to work on documents at the same time.
- When placed on an **electronic whiteboard,** drawings or information written on its surface can be displayed simultaneously on team members' computer screens.

TOOLS FOR COMMUNICATING REMOTELY

Technology networks have placed the world at our fingertips. To exploit the possibilities, whole new channels for communication have emerged.

CELLULAR TELEPHONE

- Mobile phones or cell phones are cellular radios that transmit messages over airways.
- Cost of equipment and service is justified by powerful communication capabilities, including voice mail, text messaging, global positioning services, etc.

PDAS

- **Personal digital assistants** (PDAs) provide computer capabilities in a portable form.
- In addition to data storage and software applications, some PDAs offer email capabilities and phone service.

EMAIL & INSTANT MESSAGING

- Email messages and attached files are distributed at the sender's convenience to an electronic mailbox to be read at the receiver's convenience.
- Instant messaging is interactive email that allows a varying number of people to log on to a "chat room" and exchange text dialog that can be seen by all logged-in participants.
- Video chat allows participants to see and hear each other as they chat.

ELECTRONIC CONFERENCES

- Teleconferencing and videoconferencing are cost-efficient alternatives to face-to-face meetings for people in different locations.
- Using collaborative software with web camera technology, users can see each other.
- Videoconferencing restores the nonverbal elements lost with telephone, email, and instant messaging.

1-5 your turn Electronic Café

Instant Messaging Joins the Workforce

Instant messaging (IM) is not just for the younger set and their social conversations. Many firms are adopting instant messaging as a legitimate and valuable business tool. About a quarter of U.S. companies use IM as an official corporate communication service, and an additional 44 percent have employees who use IM on their own.[26] In thousands of organizations, instant messaging is complementing and replacing existing media such as email and voice messages. Some corporate leaders, however, have expressed concerns over productivity and security that might be jeopardized when using IM. The following electronic activities will allow you to explore the IM phenomenon in more depth:

- *Learn how instant messaging works.* Visit your text support site at www.thomsonedu.com/bcomm/lehman, to learn more about instant messaging. From the Chapter 1 Electronic Café, you can access an online article describing how instant messaging works. Be prepared to discuss in class the features and uses of IM or follow your instructor's directions about how to use this information.

- *Read about how instant messaging can be an advantage and disadvantage at work.* Access the Business & Company Resource Center at http://bcrc.swlearning.com or another database available from your campus library to read more about the use of instant messaging in the workplace. Locate the following full-text articles:

Gurliacci, D. (2004, November 22). Instant messaging at work has drawbacks. *Fairfield County Business Journal*, p. 5.

Montague, C. (2005, January 17). Companies grapple with the pros and cons of workplace instant messaging. *Akron Beacon Journal*.

Compile a list of advantages and a list of disadvantages of using IM in the workplace.

- *Participate in an online chat.* Your instructor will give you directions about how and when to log on to your online course and participate in an online chat on the following topic: *Instant messaging can be an effective business tool if . . .*

- *Consider helpful tips for using instant messaging.* Access your text support site at www.thomsonedu.com/bcomm/lehman to find helpful tips on using instant messaging as a business communication tool.

Knowing how to "tunnel" through the vast amounts of irrelevant information available on the Internet to find what you want can be overwhelming. The experience can also be expensive in terms of human time spent and charges incurred for online time. Locating information from electronic sources requires that you know the search procedures and methods for constructing an effective search strategy. You will develop these skills when studying the research process in Chapter 9.

Effective use of various communication technologies helps ensure timely, targeted messages and responses and helps to build interpersonal relationships. This responsiveness leads to positive interactions with colleagues and strong customer commitment.

Legal and Ethical Implications of Technology

In addition to its many benefits, technology poses some challenges for the business communicator. For instance, technology raises issues of ownership, as in the case of difficulties that arise in protecting the copyright of documents transmitted over the Internet. Technology poses dilemmas over access, that is, who has the right to certain stored information pertaining to an individual or a company.

Have you personally been affected by a loss of privacy because of technology? If so, how?

Technology threatens our individual privacy, our right to be left alone, free from surveillance or interference from other individuals or organizations. Common invasions of privacy caused by technology include

- collecting excessive amounts of information for decision making and maintaining too many files.

- monitoring the exact time employees spend on a specific task and between tasks and the exact number and length of breaks, and supervisors' or coworkers' reading of another employee's electronic mail and computer files.

- integrating computer files containing information collected from more than one agency without permission.[27]

The privacy issue is explored further in the accompanying Strategic Forces feature, "Is Anything Private Anymore?"

Team Environment as a Strategic Force Influencing Communication

A team-oriented approach is replacing the traditional top-down management style in today's organizations. Firms around the world are facing problems in decreasing productivity, faltering product quality, and worker dissatisfaction. Work teams are being examined as a way to help firms remain globally competitive. Although worker involvement in the management process has long been the hallmark of Japanese business, many U.S. businesses, as well as those of other countries, are experimenting with self-directed work teams.[28] The list of companies using self-directed work teams is diverse, including such firms as Hunt-Wesson, the Internal Revenue Service, and the San Diego Zoo. Other companies using the team concept include Hewlett-Packard, Southwest Airlines, Toyota, Motorola, General Electric, and Corning.

Work Team Defined

The terms *team, work team, group, work group, cross-functional team,* and *self-directed team* are often used interchangeably.[29] Whatever the title, a **team** is a small number of people with complementary skills who work together for a common purpose. Team members set their own goals, in cooperation with management, and plan how to achieve those goals and how their work is to be accomplished. The central organizing element of a team is that it has a common purpose and measurable goals for which the team can be held accountable, independent of its individual members. Employees in a self-directed work team handle a wide array of functions and work with a minimum of direct supervision.[30] Some major strengths of teams are as follows:[31]

- Teams make workers happier by causing them to feel that they are shaping their own jobs.

- Teams increase efficiency by eliminating layers of managers whose job was once to pass orders downward.

Synergy can be mathematically defined as 1 + 1 = 3.

- Teams enable a company to draw on the skills and imagination of a whole workforce. A key element in team success is the concept of **synergy**, defined as a situation in which the whole is greater than the sum of the parts. Teams provide

LEGAL & ETHICAL CONSTRAINTS

Is Anything Private Anymore?

We all live in the Internet society, whether or not we spend any time online. For most people the convenience of email, mobile phones, and voice mail has proved irresistible, but many have also begun to feel the downside of cyber vulnerability. The expanding power of electronic technology makes it possible for information to be shared globally with little effort, with or without the knowledge of the information's owner. Passage of the USA Patriot Act following the attacks of September 11, 2001, initiated new federal safety measures that many feel further endanger constitutional rights to privacy. Despite the passage of federal legislation and additional state laws designed to enhance and strengthen electronic privacy, most Americans feel they have less privacy today than ever. According to a recent Harris poll, 76 percent of Americans believe they have lost all control over personal information, and 67 percent believe that computers must be restricted in the future to preserve privacy.[32] Workplace privacy has also become an area

of concern, as computer monitoring and surveillance capabilities expand.

George Orwell, in his classic novel *1984*, described what many believe to be the ultimate in privacy-shattering totalitarianism as he offered a foreboding look at future society. In his fictitious account ". . . there was of course no way of knowing whether you were being watched at any given moment. . . . It was even conceivable that they watched everybody all the time. . . . You had to live—did live—from habit that became instinct in the assumption that every sound you made was overheard, and, except in darkness, every movement scrutinized."[33] We have now advanced technologically to the point that, if desired, this kind of surveillance is easily possible, even in darkness.

An important aspect of technology is its seductive power: If a technology exists, it must be used. Where does this principle leave the individual regarding privacy needs in a highly automated world? Experts in the area of individual privacy have suggested three key aspects in the

ethical management of information and protection of privacy:[34]

- **Relevance**

An inquiring party should have a clear and valid purpose for delving into the information of an individual.

- **Consent**

An individual should be given the right to withhold consent prior to any query that might violate privacy.

- **Methods**

An inquiring party should distinguish between methods of inquiry that are reasonable and customary and those that are of questionable ethical grounding.

While technology offers tremendous advantages and endless possibilities for enhancing communication, it poses challenges for both individuals and organizations in the maintenance of a proper degree of privacy. Most of us are not ready for the all-seeing eye of Orwell's "Big Brother."

Application

Read a book review of George Orwell's *1984*. In a two-page written summary, cite instances in which Orwell described futuristic technological capabilities that have been realized in recent years. How has society's response to these capabilities differed from the fictional plot?

Ziggy

The concept of synergy is that the whole is greater than the sum of the parts.

a depth of expertise that is unavailable at the individual level, as illustrated in the Ziggy cartoon. Teams open lines of communication that then lead to increased interaction among employees and between employees and management. The result is that teams help companies reach their goals of delivering higher-quality products and services faster and with more cost effectiveness.

Communication Differences in Work Teams

> *Team function can be deterred by emotional, process, and cultural barriers.*

In the past most businesses were operated in a hierarchical fashion, with most decisions made at the top and communication following a top-down/bottom-up pattern. Communication patterns are different in successful team environments as compared to traditional organizational structures:

- Trust building is the primary factor that changes the organization's communication patterns.
- Open meetings are an important method for enhancing communication, as they educate employees about the business while building bridges of understanding and trust.
- Shared leadership, which involves more direct and effective communication between management and its internal customers, is common.
- Listening, problem solving, conflict resolution, negotiation, and consensus become important factors in group communication.
- Information flows vertically up to management and down to workers, as well as horizontally among team members, other teams, and supervisors.

Communication is perhaps the single most important aspect of successful teamwork. Open lines of communication increase interaction between employees and management. All affected parties should be kept informed as projects progress.

Maximization of Work Team Effectiveness

Grouping employees into a team structure does not mean that they will automatically function as a team. A group must go through a developmental process to begin to function as a team. Members need training in such areas as problem solving, goal setting, and conflict resolution. Teams must be encouraged to establish the "three R's"—roles, rules, and relationships.[35]

What do you see as the three major challenges to the success of work teams?

The self-directed work team can become the basic organizational building block to best ensure success in dynamic global competition. Skills for successful participation in team environments are somewhat different from those necessary for success in old-style organizations:

- The ability to give and take constructive criticism, listen actively, clearly impart one's views to others, and provide meaningful feedback are important to the success of work teams.

- Emotional barriers, such as insecurity or condescension, can limit team effectiveness.

- Removal of process barriers, such as rigid policies and procedures, can also interfere by stifling effective team functioning.

- Cultural barriers, such as stereotyped roles and responsibilities, can separate workers from management.[36] Understanding of the feelings and needs of coworkers is needed so that members feel comfortable stating their opinions and discussing the strengths and weaknesses of the team.

- The emergence of leadership skills that apply to a dynamic group setting lead to team success. In the dynamic team leadership, referred to as **distributed leadership**, the role of leader may alternate among members, and more than one leadership style may be active at any given time.[37]

To improve group communication, time needs to be set aside to assess the quality of interaction. Questions to pose about the group process might include the following:

- What are our common goals?

- What roles are members playing? For instance, is one person dominating while others contribute little or nothing?

- Is the group dealing with conflict in a positive way?

- What in the group process is going well?

- What about the group process could be improved?

Gender, cultural, and age differences among members of a team can present barriers to team communication. Knowing what behaviors may limit the group process is imperative to maximizing results. Team members may need awareness training to assist in recognizing behaviors that may hinder team performance and in overcoming barriers that may limit the effectiveness of their communication. You can explore the team model versus reward for individual effort by completing the Case Analysis at the end of this chapter. *Building High-Performance Teams,* a handbook that accompanies this text, will guide you through the stages of team development and various collaborative processes as you pursue a team-based class project.

Communicating Internationally Looms as a CDC Challenge

The Centers for Disease Control (CDC) is charged with the responsibility of protecting the health and safety of people at home and abroad. The agency develops and provides disease control information and distributes it to enhance healthy decisions and behaviors. Communicaton with other health partners as well as the public is essential to ensuring the health of the people of the United States and elsewhere in the world.

Julie Gerberding, director of the CDC, has acknowledged the challenge of balancing the urgent goal of preparing for a bioterrorism emergency with the agency's fundamental mission of preventing and controlling infectious diseases and other health hazards. According to Gerberding, "HIV right now is the overwhelming global epidemic. To not put that on the front burner would

simply be a sign of no credibility at all. We have some programs that work and we need to get them out there."[38]

© Gregory Smith/AP Photo

- Visit the CDC website at http://www.cdc.gov and read the organization's mission statement. What aspects of the CDC's mission focus on communication?

- Locate the following article through the Business & Company Resource Center at http://bcrc.swlearning.com that describes efforts of the CDC to educate people about their HIV status:

  CDC hunts for firm to direct three HIV prevention efforts. (2004, August 9). *PR Week*, 3.

Activities

1. Refer to the Communication Process Model presented in Figure 1-1. In a class discussion, identify barriers that the CDC might experience in communicating its AIDS

campaign to people in various subcultures.

2. The CDC TV ads to get 9- to 13-year-olds off their duffs and into exercise focus on the value of a healthy lifestyle instead of the dangers of obesity. Read the following article found in Business & Company Resource Center that describes the positive advertising communication strategy:

Many kids are aware of CDC obesity campaign. (2004, March 21). *Medical Letter on the CDC & FDA*, 59.

Consider the information presented in this chapter about intergenerational communication issues. Prepare a three-column chart that shows reasons to avoid obesity that might appeal to persons ages 12, 25, and 50.

http://www.cdc.gov

Summary

1. **Define communication and describe the main purposes for communication in business.**

   Communication is the process of exchanging information and meaning between or among individuals through a common system of symbols, signs, and behavior. Managers spend most of their time in communication activities.

2. **Explain the communication process model and the ultimate objective of the communication process.**

   People engaged in communication encode and decode messages while simultaneously serving as both senders and receivers. In the communication process, feedback helps people resolve possible misunderstandings and thus improve communication effectiveness. Feedback and the opportunity to observe nonverbal signs are always present in face-to-face communication, the most complete of the three communication levels.

3. **Discuss how information flows within an organization (through various levels; formally and informally; and downward, upward, and horizontally).**

   Communication takes place at five levels: intrapersonal (communication within one person), interpersonal (communication between two people), group (communication among more than two people), organizational (communication among combinations of groups), and public (communication from one entity to the greater public). Both formal and informal communication systems exist in every organization; the formal system exists to accomplish tasks, and the informal system serves a personal maintenance purpose that results in people feeling better about themselves and others. Communication flows upward, downward, and horizontally or laterally. These flows often defy formal graphic description, yet each is a necessary part of the overall communication activity of the organization.

4. **Explain how legal and ethical constraints, diversity challenges, changing technology, and team environment act as strategic forces that influence the process of business communication.**

   Communication occurs within an environment constrained by legal and ethical requirements, diversity challenges, changing technology, and team environment requirements.

   - International, federal, state, and local laws impose legal boundaries for business activity, and ethical boundaries are determined by personal analysis that can be assisted by application of various frameworks for decision making.

   - Communication is critically impacted by diversity in nationality, culture, age, gender, and other factors that offer tremendous opportunities to maximize talent, ideas, and productivity but pose significant challenges in interpretation of time, personal space requirements, body language, and language translation.

   - Significant strides have occurred in the development of tools for data collection and analysis, shaping messages to be clearer and more effective, and communicating quickly and efficiently over long distances. The use of technology, however, poses legal and ethical concerns in regard to ownership, access, and privacy.

   - Team environment challenges arise because communication in teams differs from communication in traditional organizational structures. The result of effective teams is better decisions, more creative solutions to problems, and higher worker morale.

Chapter Review

1. What are the three purposes for which people communicate? What percentage of a manager's time is spent communicating? Give examples of the types of communication managers use. (Obj. 1)

2. Describe the five stages in the communication process using the following terms: (a) sender, (b) encode, (c) channel, (d) receiver, (e) decode, (f) feedback, and (g) interferences or barriers. (Obj. 2)

3. What is the difference between intrapersonal and interpersonal communication? (Obj. 3)

4. How is the formal flow of communication different from the informal flow of communication? (Obj. 3)

5. What are some common causes of unethical behavior in the workplace? (Obj. 4)

6. Describe several intercultural communication barriers and how they might be overcome. (Obj. 4)

7. Describe several ways that communication technology can assist individuals and organizations. (Obj. 4)

8. What legal and ethical concerns are raised over the use of technology? (Obj. 4)

9. How does communication in work teams differ from that of traditional organizations? (Obj. 4)

10. Why has communication been identified as perhaps the single most important aspect of team work? (Obj. 4)

Digging Deeper

1. What aspect of cultural diversity do you feel will impact you most in your career: international, intercultural, intergenerational, or gender? Explain your answer, including how you plan to deal with the challenge.

2. Lack of Internet access is causing some nations to be classified as information "have nots." What international communication problems could result?

3. Considering the four strategic forces discussed, how is business communication today different from that of 30 years ago? In what ways is it easier? In what ways is it more difficult?

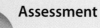

Assessment

To check your understanding of the chapter, take the available online quizzes as directed by your instructor.

Activities

1. **Shadowing a Manager's Communication Activities (Obj. 1)**

   Shadow a business manager for a day. Keep a log of his/her communication activities for the time period you are observing. Divide the communication activities into the following categories: (1) attending meetings, (2) presenting information to groups, (3) explaining procedures and work assignments, (4) coordinating the work of various employees and departments, (5) evaluating and counseling employees, (6) promoting the company's products/services and image, and (7) other activities. Calculate the percentage of time spent in each activity. Be prepared to share your results with the class.

2. **Clocking Your Own Communication Activities (Obj. 1)**

   Prepare a record of your listening, speaking, reading, and writing activities and time spent in each during the hours of 8 a.m. to 5 p.m. for the next two days. You should attempt to record the time spent doing each activity for each one-hour time block in such a way that you obtain a total time for each activity. Be prepared to share your distribution with the class.

3. **Communication Barriers (Obj. 2)**

   In groups of three, develop a list of 10 to 12 annoying habits of yours or of others that create barriers (verbal and nonverbal) to effective communication. Classify each according to the portion of the communication process it affects. For each, give at least one suggestion for improvement. Access a downloadable version of this activity from the text support site (www.thomsonedu.com/bcomm/lehman).

4. **Organizational Communication Flows (Obj. 3)**

   Draw an organizational chart to depict the formal system of communication within an organization with which you are familiar. How is the informal system different from the organization chart? How are the five levels of communication achieved in the organization? Be prepared to discuss these points in class.

5. **Identifying Ethical Dilemmas (Obj. 4)**

   Using an online index, locate a current newspaper or magazine article that describes an illegal or unethical act by a business organization or its employee(s). Choose an incident as closely related as possible to your intended profession. Be prepared to share details of the incident in an informal presentation to the class.

6. **Diversity Challenges as a Strategic Force (Obj. 4)**

   Conduct an online search to locate examples of intercultural communication mistakes made by U.S. companies doing business in another country. How can an organization improve its diversity awareness to avoid such problems? Be prepared to share your ideas with the class.

7. **Classroom Diversity Initiative (Obj. 4)**

   In your class, locate other students to form a "diverse" group; your diversity may include age (more than five years difference), gender, race, culture, geographic origin, etc. Discuss your areas of diversity; then identify three things the group members all have in common, excluding your school experience. Share your group experiences with the class.

8. **Changing Technology as a Strategic Force (Objs. 2, 4)**

   Indicate which of the following communication mediums would be most appropriate for sending the following messages: email, fax, telephone, or face-to-face communication. Justify your answer.

   a. The company is expecting a visit from members of a committee evaluating your bid for this year's Malcolm Baldrige National Quality Award. All employees must be notified of the visit.

   b. After careful deliberation, the management of a mid-sized pharmaceutical company is convinced the only way to continue its current level of research is to sell the company to a larger one. The employees must be informed of this decision.

   c. Lincoln Enterprises is eager to receive the results of a drug test on a certain employee. The drug-testing company has been asked to send the results as quickly as possible.

   d. The shipping department has located the common carrier currently holding a customer's shipment that should have been delivered yesterday. Inform the customer that the carrier has promised delivery by tomorrow morning.

   e. An employee in another division office has requested you send a spreadsheet you have prepared so he can manipulate the data to produce a report.

9. **Technology's Impact on Communication (Obj. 4)**

   In pairs, read and discuss an article from a current magazine or journal about how technology is impacting communication. Send your instructor a brief email message discussing the major theme of the article. Include a complete bibliographic entry so the instructor can locate the article (refer to Appendix B for examples of formatted references). Your instructor will provide directions for setting up an email account and composing and sending an email message.

10. **Exploring Use of Teams in the Workplace (Obj. 4)**

    Using the Internet, locate an article that describes how a company or organization is using teams in its operation. Write a one-page abstract of the article.

Applications

Read | Think | Write | Speak | Collaborate

1. Communication Challenges in the Future Workplace (Objs. 1–4)

Locate the following article through Business & Company Resource Center (http://bcrc.swlearning.com) or another online database:

Kaplan-Leiserson, E. (2004, February). 2004 forecast. *T & D, 58*(2), 12(3).

In small groups, discuss the following:

a. What communication trends are predicted in the workplace? Are any of these surprising? Why?

b. Which trends are likely to impact your chosen career field most significantly? In what ways?

c. How do the predicted trends relate to the four strategic forces presented in this chapter?

Select one of the resource sites provided in the article. Visit the site and prepare a brief presentation to be given to the class about the trend.

2. Legal and Ethical Constraints as a Strategic Force (Obj. 4)

Read *The Power of Ethical Management* by Kenneth Blanchard and Norman Vincent Peale, a short, engaging story of a sales manager's attempt to make an ethical decision. Write a brief report summarizing the ethical principles presented in the book.

Read | **Think** | Write | Speak | Collaborate

3. Analyzing an Ethical Dilemma (Obj. 4)

Locate the following article available in full text from Business & Company Resource Center http://bcrc.swlearning.com or from another database available through your campus library:

Dubinsky, J. E. (2002, October). When an employee question presents an ethical dilemma. *Payroll Manager's Report,* 1.

After reading the article, refer to the text support site (www.thomsonedu.com/bcomm/lehman) for informa-

tion on other ethical frameworks. Respond to the following questions.

a. Who are the stakeholders in the case? What does each stand to gain or lose, depending on your decision?

b. How does the situation described in the case relate to the four-dimension model shown in Figure 1-7?

c. What factors might influence your decision as the manager in the case?

d. How would *you* respond to the employee in the case? Why?

Read | Think | **Write** | Speak | Collaborate

4. Writing About Your Team Orientation (Obj. 4)

Effective teamwork is important to many career paths. Take the team player quiz at the Monster career site

Write a brief paper about your team orientation and how being a team player may affect your career success.

Read | Think | Write | **Speak** | Collaborate

5. Understanding Diversity Issues (Obj. 4)

Read the discussion of "Culture and Communication" at the text support site (www.thomsonedu.com/bcomm/lehman). In groups of three, interview an international student at your institution and generate a list of English words

that have no equivalents in his or her language. Find out about nonverbal communication that may differ from that used in American culture. Share your findings in a short presentation to the class.

6. So Many Ways to Fail (Obj. 1-2)

Locate the following article available in full text from Business & Company Resource Center http://bcrc. swlearning.com or from another database available through your campus library:

Olsztynski, J. (2006). Failures to communicate: Why they happened; how to make sure they don't. *National Driller, 20*(2), 14(3).

Summarize briefly the five reasons for communication failures in the workplace described in this article and suggestions for correcting them. Discuss experiences where "communication failure" was blamed for problems that occurred in your work, academic, or personal interactions. From your discussions generate three to five additional ways communication can fail with suggestions for correcting them. Present to the class in a short presentation.

Case Analysis

Can the United States Succeed Without Rewarding Rugged Individuality?

A basic element of the fabric of U.S. entrepreneurship is the faith in the ingenuity of the individual person's ability to conceive, develop, and profit from a business endeavor. The frontier spirit and triumph of the individual over looming odds have been a predominant force in the development of the United States. Such individualism has also been recognized by organizations, with reward going to those who contribute winning ideas and efforts.

The recent shift in organizational structures toward team design has caused management to reassess reward systems that focus on individual recognition and to consider rewards that are based on team performance. Some fear that removing individual incentive will lead to mediocrity and a reduction in personal effort. They argue that while the team model might work in other cultures, it is inconsistent with the U.S. way of thinking and living. According to Madelyn Hoshstein, president of DYG Inc., a New

York firm that researches corporate trends, America is moving away from the model of team building in which everyone is expected to do everything and toward focusing on employees who are the best at what they do. She describes this change as a shift toward social Darwinism and away from egalitarianism, in which everyone has equal economic, political, and social rights.[39]

Team advocates say that teams are here to stay and liken those who deny that reality to the proverbial ostrich with its head in the sand. They stress the need for newly structured incentive plans to reward group effort.

Visit the text support site at www.thomsonedu.com/ bcomm/lehman to link to web resources related to this topic. Respond to one or more of the following activities, as directed by your instructor.

1. GMAT How would you respond to those with concerns about loss of individual incentive? Argue for or against the increased emphasis on team reward, using either personal examples or examples from business.

2. Structure a reward system that would recognize both individual and team performance. You may use an organization of your choice to illustrate.

3. Select a specific corporation or nation that has implemented the team model. Describe the transition away from a hierarchical structure and the consequences that have resulted from the shift, both positive and negative.

Chapter 2
Focusing on Interpersonal and Group Communication

Objectives

When you have completed Chapter 2, you will be able to:

1 Explain how behavioral theories about human needs, trust and disclosure, and motivation relate to business communication.

2 Describe the role of nonverbal messages in communication.

3 Identify aspects of effective listening.

4 Identify factors affecting group and team communication.

5 Discuss aspects of effective meeting management.

©/AP Graphics Bank

eBay Connects a Worldwide Market

Growing faster in its first decade than any other enterprise in the history of capitalism, eBay has exploded as a global online marketplace connecting buyers and sellers 24/7. Founded in 1995, eBay now conducts more transactions every day than the Nasdaq Stock Market and has annual revenues of more than $4 billion.[1] In the 1990s, people thought e-commerce would be dominated by big players, but instead the last decade has produced a market driven by individuals and small businesses.

Nearly 160 million registered users in 33 markets can scan 55 million items at any time, and about $1,400 worth of goods are traded on the site every second.[2] eBay has also created jobs, with more than 724,000 Americans saying they earn all or most of their income selling goods online through eBay.[3] The site has provided people with the opportunity to start their own businesses at reduced costs by using eBay to buy needed equipment and to sell their goods.

Founder and chairman, Pierre Omidyar, acknowledges that running eBay has never been just about managing employees. It's also about guiding and understanding the ever-growing community of eBay sellers. eBay is known for listening to its customers. The company's feedback system allows buyers and sellers to evaluate each other based on the quality of their dealings. PayPal, the part of eBay that allows individual sellers to accept credit card payments, was a direct result of customer demand; in the near future, eBay listings, which are now static web pages, will have sound and video.

> *Millions of people have learned that they can trust a complete stranger. That's had an incredible social impact. People have more in common than they think.*

EBay continues to expand worldwide. In about 15 percent of current transactions, the buyer and seller are in different countries. With this ratio steadily increasing, eBay has a tremendous power to connect the Third World with the industrialized world. Omidyar says that the most significant lesson demonstrated by eBay is "the remarkable fact that millions of people have learned that they can trust a complete stranger. That's had an incredible social impact. People have more in common than they think."[4] To be effective in the ever-changing environment of business, you will need to have an understanding of human behavior and its influences on organizational and group communication.

http://www.ebay.com

SEE SHOWCASE, PART 2, ON PAGE 48, FOR SPOTLIGHT COMMUNICATOR MEG WHITMAN, CEO OF EBAY.

Behavioral Theories that Impact Communication

Objective 1

Explain how behavioral theories about human needs, trust and disclosure, and motivation relate to business communication.

Behavioral scientists working in the fields of sociology and psychology have strongly influenced business management by focusing on the complexities of communication in the work environment. An understanding of human needs and motivation provides a supervisor with valuable insights that facilitate effective communication with and among employees.

Recognizing Human Needs

Psychologist Abraham Maslow developed the concept of a hierarchy of needs through which people progress. In our society, most people have reasonably satisfied their two lower levels of needs: (1) physiological needs (food and basic provision) and (2) their security and safety needs (shelter and protection from the elements and physical danger). Beyond these two basic need levels, people progress to satisfy the three upper levels: (3) social needs for love, acceptance, and belonging; (4) ego or esteem needs to be heard, appreciated, and wanted; and (5) self-actualizing needs, including the need to achieve one's fullest potential through professional, philanthropic, political, educational, and artistic channels.

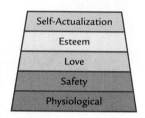

As people satisfy needs at one level, they move on to the next. The levels that have been satisfied still are present, but their importance diminishes. Effective communicators are able to identify and appeal to need levels in various individuals or groups. Advertising is designed to appeal to need levels. Luxury car ads appeal to ego needs, teeth whitening and deodorant ads appeal to social needs, and cellular telephone and home security system ads appeal to security and safety needs. In business, efforts to help people satisfy needs are essential, since a satisfied worker is generally more productive than a dissatisfied one. In communication activities, a sender's message is more likely to appeal to the receiver if the receiver's need is accurately identified.

To which need level would each of the following apply: private office, years of service award, expanded retirement program, health and fitness programs?

Southwest Airlines promotes an environment of mutual trust by empowering employees at all levels to make decisions that are vital to their effective job performance.

© Comstock Images/Jupiter Images

Stroking

People engage in communication with others in the hope that the outcome may lead to mutual trust, mutual pleasure, and psychological well-being. The communication exchange is a means of sharing information about things, ideas, tasks, and selves.

Each communication interaction, whether casual or formal, provides an emotional **stroke** that may have either a positive or a negative effect on your feelings about yourself and others. Getting a pat on the back from the supervisor, receiving a congratulatory telephone call or letter, and being listened to by another person are examples of everyday positive strokes. Negative strokes might include receiving a hurtful comment, being avoided or left out of conversation, and getting reprimanded by a superior. By paying attention to the importance of strokes, managers can greatly improve communication and people's feelings about their work.

Exploring the Johari Window

Think about the types of information you (1) share freely, (2) share only with close friends, and (3) keep hidden. How do these decisions affect your interpersonal communication?

As relationships develop, the people involved continue to learn about each other and themselves, as shown by the Johari Window in Figure 2-1. Area I, the free or open area, represents what we know about ourselves and what others know about us. Area II, the blind area, designates those things others know about us but that we don't know about ourselves; for example, you are the only person who can't see your physical self as it really is. Things we know about ourselves but that others don't know about us occupy the hidden or secret area III. Area IV includes the unknown: things we don't know about ourselves and others don't know about us, such as our ability to handle emergency situations if we've never been faced with them.

Each of the window areas may vary in size according to the degree to which we learn about ourselves and are willing to disclose things about ourselves to others. Reciprocal sharing occurs when people develop *trust* in each other. When a confidant

Figure 2-1 | **The Johari Window**

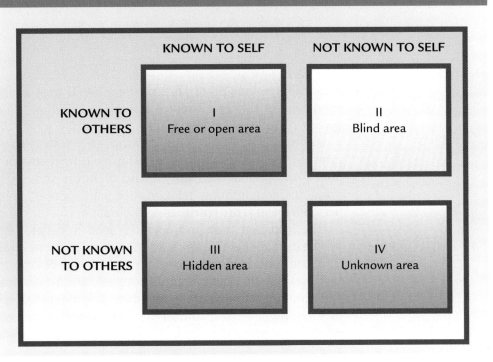

Secure Email Protects Corporate Information

Organizations need secure control over incoming and outgoing email. Health care providers must make sure patient privacy is protected, and financial and governmental institutions must provide similar safeguards for their sensitive data. Regulations may also require that certain types of information be transmitted through email only in an encrypted form. A number of vendors offer software solutions for managing secure messaging so that the receiver doesn't know anything is different. Various software firms offer products that help secure organizations' borders against unwanted intrusion into their email. The following electronic activities will allow you to explore the topic of secure email in more depth:

Learn more about secure email systems. Visit your text support site at www.thomsonedu.com/bcomm/lehman to learn more about secure email systems. Refer to Chapter 2's Electronic Café activity that provides links to an online article that discusses the value of corporate email policies in protecting against confidentiality breaches. Be prepared to discuss this information or use it as directed by your instructor.

Read about email security products. Access Business & Company Resource Center at http://bcrc.swlearning.com or another database available from your campus library to read more about several products that offer email security solutions. Search for the following article that is available in full text:

Schultz, K. (2004, September 20). Clash of the email encryptors: Email security solutions from PGP, PostX, Sigaba, and Tumbleweed compete on flexibility, power, and ease. InfoWorld, 26(38), p. 21.

Message using secure email. Your instructor will give you directions about how to use the secure email provided through your online course. In WebTutor, email your instructor or another student in your class, describing a business situation that would require a secure email transaction.

Learn more about security. Access your text support site (www.thomsonedu.com/bcomm/lehman) for five lessons on email security.

---

demonstrates that he or she can be trusted, trust is reinforced and leads to an expansion of the open area of the Johari Window. We are usually willing to tell people about various things that aren't truly personal. But we share personal thoughts, ambitions, and inner feelings only with selected others—those whom we have learned to trust. The relationships existing between supervisor and employee, doctor and patient, and lawyer and client are those of trust, but only in specific areas. In more intimate relationships with spouses, siblings, and parents, deeper, personal feelings are entrusted to each other.

Trust is earned over time through consistent behaviors.

The idea that trust and openness lead to better communication between two people also applies to groups. Managers engaged in **organizational development** (OD) are concerned with developing successful organizations by building effective small groups. They believe small group effectiveness evolves mostly from a high level of mutual trust among group members. The aim of OD is to open emotional as well as task-oriented communication. To accomplish this aim, groups often become involved in encounter sessions designed to enlarge the open areas of the Johari Window.[5]

your turn · You're the Professional

You have just learned that you were selected to fill the position as department manager in a company with which you interviewed. Ms. Blake, the previous manager, was well liked; but productivity in the department was considerably below what your supervisor desires it to be. You plan to call a meeting with your staff on your first day at work. Which of the following will be the theme of your presentation?

1. I'm not Ms. Blake, so some things will be different around here.

2. We will get along fine if everyone does his/her work well.

3. This is a great department, and together we can make it better.

4. Productivity is a problem that together we must address.

Describe the reason for your choice and other ideas that you might include in your presentation.

Contrasting Management Styles

Douglas McGregor, a management theorist, attempted to distinguish between the older, traditional view that workers are concerned only about satisfying lower-level needs and the more contemporary view that productivity can be enhanced by assisting workers in satisfying higher-level needs. Under the older view, management exercised strong control, emphasized the job to the exclusion of concern for the individual, and sought to motivate solely through external incentives—a job and a paycheck. McGregor labeled this management style Theory X. Under the contemporary style, Theory Y, management strives to balance control and individual freedom. By treating the individual as a mature person, management lessens the need for external motivation; treated as adults, people will act as adults.

The situational leadership model developed by Paul Hersey and Kenneth Blanchard does not prescribe a single leadership style, but advocates that what is appropriate in each case depends on the follower (subordinate) and the task to be performed. **Directive behavior** is characterized by the leader's giving detailed rules and instructions and monitoring closely that they are followed. The leader decides what is to be done and how. In contrast, **supportive behavior** is characterized by the leader's listening, communicating, recognizing, and encouraging. Different degrees of directive and supportive behavior can be desirable, given the situation.[6] Combining the ideas of Maslow and McGregor with those of Hersey and Blanchard leads to the conclusion that "the right job for the person" is a better philosophy than "the right person for the job."

The **Total Quality Management** movement focuses on creating a more responsible role for the worker in an organization. In a Total Quality Management environment, decision-making power is distributed to the people closest to the problem, those who usually have the best information sources and solutions. Each employee, from the president to the custodian, is expected to solve problems, participate in team-building efforts, and expand the scope of his or her role in the organization. The goal of employee empowerment is to build a work environment in which all employees take pride in their work accomplishments and begin motivating themselves from within rather than through traditional extrinsic

TEAM ENVIRONMENT

Spotlight Communicator:
Meg Whitman
CEO OF EBAY

"The Power of Us" Fuels Company Success

Meg Whitman had never even heard of eBay when she agreed to interview. She hoped her headhunter would call back with something more promising. Little did she know that the firm she had never heard of would become one of history's fastest growing companies with her at its helm. Since Meg Whitman joined eBay as CEO in 1998, revenues have exploded, and eBay has become a household word throughout much of the world. Under her democratic leadership, the collective intelligence and enthusiasm of 160 million customers determine and drive the daily actions of the company's 9,300 employees. "At eBay, it's a collaborative network. You are truly in partnership with the community of users. The key is connecting employees and customers in two-way communication. We call it "The Power of Us."[7]

A key belief underlying Whitman's leadership is that people are basically good and can be trusted. A second of her guiding principles for management is to never assume you know more than the marketplace or community, because you don't. To learn more about the growing community of Chinese Internet users, Whitman has made several trips to China, listening and trying to understand how the country actually works.

It's debatable as to whether great leaders are born or bred, and in Whitman's case the mystery continues. Following completion of an MBA at Harvard, Whitman began her career in brand management at Procter & Gamble, where she learned to always put the customer first. Through holding positions with several other firms before joining eBay, including Bain, Disney, StrideRite, and Hasbro, Whitman learned how to get things done in places where she was not well known or well established. This required listening, learning, collaboration, and building business relationships. She credits Disney's late president and chief operating officer, Frank Wells, with teaching her the importance of executive humility.

Although nurturing, no one mistakes Whitman's sensitivity for weakness. In fact, she is a strong believer in maintaining boundaries. An example is her decision to ban the sale of weapons on eBay. According to Tom Tierney, eBay director, "Meg is a hybrid, and that's the model for the future, a decisive general manager with an open-minded influencer."[8] In 2004, *The Wall Street Journal* and CNBC recognized Meg Whitman's unusual talent by naming her as the business leader of the future; and in the same year, FORTUNE named her the most powerful woman in American business. Whitman sums up her leadership philosophy simply: "Executive leadership is a span of influence, not of control."[9]

> *The key is connecting employees and customers in two-way communication. We call it "The Power of Us."*

Applying What You Have Learned

1. Explain what Meg Whitman means by "The Power of Us."

2. What factors contributed to the leadership style exhibited by Whitman?

3. What does "executive humility" mean?

SEE SHOWCASE, PART 3, ON PAGE 66, TO EXPAND YOUR KNOWLEDGE ABOUT COMMUNICATION AT EBAY.

Appropriate attire sends a strong and positive nonverbal signal.

incentives.[10] Managers of many companies understand that empowering employees to initiate continuous improvements is critical for survival. Only companies producing quality products and services will survive in today's world market.

Nonverbal Communication

Objective 2
Describe the role of nonverbal messages in communication.

Managers use verbal and nonverbal messages to communicate an idea to a recipient. Verbal means "through the use of words," either written or spoken. Nonverbal means "without the use of words." Although major attention in communication study is given to verbal messages, studies show that nonverbal messages can account for over 90 percent of the total meaning.[11] Nonverbal communication includes *metacommunication* and *kinesic* messages.

Metacommunication

A **metacommunication** is a message that, although *not* expressed in words, accompanies a message that *is* expressed in words. For example, "Don't be late for work" communicates caution; yet the sentence may imply (but not express in words) such additional ideas as "You are frequently late, and I'm warning you," or "I doubt your dependability" (metacommunication). "Your solution is perfect" may also convey a metacommunication such as "You are efficient," or "I certainly like your work." Whether you are speaking or writing, you can be confident that those who receive your messages will be sensitive to the messages expressed in words and to the accompanying messages that are present but not expressed in words.

Kinesic Messages

What nonverbal messages might be conveyed by a job applicant? A customer? A salesperson?

People constantly send meaning through kinesic communication, an idea expressed through nonverbal behavior. In other words, receivers gain additional meaning from what they see and hear—the visual and the vocal:

- **Visual**—gestures, winks, smiles, frowns, sighs, attire, grooming, and all kinds of body movements.

- **Vocal**—intonation, projection, and resonance of the voice.

Some examples of kinesic messages and the meanings they may convey follow.

Action	Possible Kinesic Message
A wink or light chuckle follows a statement.	*"Don't believe what I just said."*
A manager is habitually late for staff meetings.	*"My time is more important than yours. You can wait for me." Alternately, the action may be ordinary for a non-U.S. born manager.*
A supervisor lightly links his arm around an employee's shoulders at the end of a formal disciplinary conference.	*"Everything is fine; I'm here to help you solve this problem." Alternately, the action may be sexually motivated or paternalistic—comforting a child after necessary discipline.*
A job applicant submits a résumé containing numerous errors.	*"My language skills are deficient." Alternately, "I didn't care to do my best."*
The supervisor looks up but then returns her attention to a current project when an employee arrives for a performance appraisal interview.	*"The performance appraisal interview is not an important process. You are interrupting more important work."*
A group leader sits at a position other than at the head of the table.	*"I want to demonstrate my equality with other members."*
An employee's clothing does not comply with the company's dress code.	*"Rules are for other people; I can do what I want." Alternately, "I do not understand the expectations."*
A manager hesitates when asked to justify a new rule for employees.	*"I don't have a good reason." Alternately, "I want to think this through to be sure I give an understandable answer."*

What nonverbal messages did you convey today through your attire, posture, gestures, etc?

Understanding Nonverbal Messages

Metacommunications and kinesic communications have characteristics that all communicators should take into account.

- **Nonverbal messages cannot be avoided.** Both written and spoken words convey ideas in addition to the ideas contained in the words used. All actions—and even the lack of action—have meaning to those who observe them.

- **Nonverbal messages may have different meanings for different people.** If a team member smiles after making a statement, one member may conclude that the speaker was trying to be funny; another may conclude that the speaker was pleased about having made such a great contribution; another may see the smile as indicating friendliness.

- **Nonverbal messages vary between and within cultures.** Not only do nonverbal messages have different meanings from culture to culture, but men and women from the same culture typically exhibit different body language. As a rule, U.S. men make less body contact with other men than do women with women. Acceptable male body language might include a handshake or a pat on the back, while women are afforded more flexibility in making body contact with each other. The accompanying Strategic Forces feature "Cultural Differences in Nonverbal Messages" provides more information on cultural differences in nonverbal communication.

Have you ever experienced a situation in which the verbal and nonverbal message did not agree? Describe it. Which message did you believe? Why?

- **Nonverbal messages may be intentional or unintentional.** "You are right about that" may be intended to mean "I agree with you" or "You are right on *this* issue, but you have been wrong on all others discussed." The sender may or may not intend to convey the latter and may or may not be aware of doing so.

- **Nonverbal messages can contradict the accompanying verbal message, and affect whether your message is understood or believed.** If the verbal and nonverbal messages contradict each other, which do you suppose the receiver will believe? The old adage "Actions speak louder than words" provides the answer. Picture a person who says, "I'm happy to be here," but looks at the floor, talks in a weak and halting voice, and clasps his hands together in front of his body in an inhibited "fig-leaf" posture. Because his verbal and nonverbal messages are contradictory, his audience may not trust his words. Similarly, consider the negative effect of a sloppy personal appearance by a job candidate.

- **Nonverbal messages may receive more attention than verbal messages.** If a supervisor rhythmically taps a pen while making a statement, the words may not register in the employee's mind. An error in basic grammar may receive more attention than the idea that is being transmitted.

- **Nonverbal messages provide clues about the sender's background and motives.** For example, excessive use of big words may suggest that a person reads widely or has an above-average education; it may also suggest a need for social recognition or insecurity about social background.

- **Nonverbal messages are influenced by the circumstances surrounding the communication.** Assume that two men, Ganesh and Sam, are friends who work for the same firm. When they are together on the job, Ganesh sometimes puts his hand on Sam's shoulder. To Sam, the act may mean nothing more than "We are close friends." But suppose Ganesh is a member of a committee that subsequently denies a promotion for Sam. Afterward, the same act could mean "We are still friends," but it could also arouse resentment. Because of the circumstances, the same act could now mean something like "Watch the hand that pats; it can also stab."

- **Nonverbal messages may be beneficial or harmful.** Words or actions can be accompanied by nonverbal messages that help or hurt the sender's purpose. Metacommunications and kinesic communications can convey something like "I am efficient in my business and considerate of others," or they can convey the opposite. They cannot be eliminated, but they can be made to work for communicators instead of against them.

FRANK & EARNEST

Effective listening skills are essential to career success.

Cultural Differences in Nonverbal Messages

International communication poses particular challenges for proper use of nonverbal signals. At the opening session of Bangladesh's new parliament in July 1996, legislators reacted with fury to a gesture by U.S. Shipping Minister A. S. M. Abdur Rob. "This is a dishonor not only to parliament but to the nation," said Dr. A. Q. M. Badruddoza Chowdhury, the Bangladesh Nationalist Party's deputy leader.

What Rob had done to provoke such anger was to give the thumbs up sign. In the United States, the gesture means "good going!" But in Bangladesh, it is a taunt; in other Islamic countries, it is an obscenity. This example is only one of the huge array of cross-cultural gaffes a naive U.S. businessperson could make on an overseas assignment.[12]

Becoming familiar with subtle and not-so-subtle differences in nonverbal communication in other cultures can avoid the barriers to effective communication. Some cultural examples of nonverbal behavior include the following:

- The Japanese greet with a respectful bow rather than the traditional handshake. Middle Easterners may exchange kisses on the cheek as the preferred form of greeting.

- While North Americans believe that eye contact is an indicator of interest and trust, the Japanese believe that lowering the eyes is a sign of respect. Asian females and many African Americans listen without direct eye contact. Extended facial gazing as is typified by the French and Brazilians is often seen by Americans as aggressive.

- The time-conscious North American can expect to be kept waiting for an appointment in Central America, the Middle East, and other countries where the

© /image100/Jupiter Images

North American sentiment that "time is money" is not accepted.

- North Americans, who often slap each other on the back or put an arm around the other as a sign of friendship, receive disapproval from the Japanese, who avoid physical contact. Japanese shopkeepers place change on a plastic plate to avoid physical contact with customers.[13]

Numerous research studies point out the importance of nonverbal communication in international negotiations. A 15-year study of negotiation styles in 17 cultures revealed that Japanese negotiators behaved least aggressively, typically using a polite conversation style with infrequent use of "no" and "you" as well as more silent periods. The style of French negotiators was most aggressive, including more threats and warnings, as well as interruptions, facial gazing, and frequent use of "no" and "you." Brazilians were similarly aggressive, with more physical touching of their negotiating partners. Germans, the British, and Americans fell somewhat in the middle.

Removing words from a negotiation might at times give the process additional strength by avoiding many of the problems raised by verbal communication in a multicultural context. The negotiation process is the sum of such factors as the number of parties, existence of external audiences, issues to be discussed, deadlines, laws, ethics, customs, physical setting, and so on. The emphasis on nonverbal cues is often lost on American negotiators who rely on the inherent advantage provided by their mastery of global languages. Cultural awareness includes both education and sensitivity concerning behaviors, expectations, and interpretations of persons with different backgrounds and experiences.[14]

Application

Interview a person from another culture or subculture to determine how his or her expectations for nonverbal behavior differ from your own. Chart three to five particular nonverbal actions and their meanings in each of the two cultures.

Listening as a Communication Skill

Objective 3
Identify aspects of effective listening.

Most managers spend a major part of their day listening and speaking with supervisors, employees, customers, and a variety of business or industry colleagues and associates. Listening commonly consumes more of business employees' time than reading, writing, and speaking combined. Listening is an interpersonal skill as critical as the skill of speaking. Effective listening is essential at Dell Computers, a company that has built its reputation on providing customers with custom computers based on individual needs.

Effective listening habits pay off in several ways:

Improved listening skills can benefit you in your career advancement.

- Good listeners are liked by others because they satisfy the basic human needs of being heard and being wanted.

- People who listen well are able to separate fact from fiction, cope effectively with false persuasion, and avoid having others use them for personal gain. In other words, good listeners don't "get taken" very often.

- Listening opens doors for ideas and thus encourages creativity.

- Effective listeners are constantly learning—gaining knowledge and skills that lead to increased job performance, advancement, and satisfaction.

- Job satisfaction increases when people know what is going on, when they are heard, and when they participate in the mutual trust that develops from good communication.

Listening depends on your abilities to receive and decode both verbal and nonverbal messages. The best-devised messages and sophisticated communication systems will not work unless people on the receiving end of spoken messages actually listen. Senders of spoken messages must assume their receivers can and will listen, just as senders of written messages must assume their receivers can and will read.

Listening for a Specific Purpose

Individuals satisfy a variety of purposes through listening: (1) interacting socially, (2) receiving information, (3) solving problems, and (4) sharing feelings with others. Each activity may call for a different style of listening or for a combination of styles.

- ***Casual listening.*** Listening for pleasure, recreation, amusement, and relaxation is casual listening. Some people play music all day long to relax the brain and mask unwanted sounds during daily routines, work periods, and daily commutes. Aspects of casual listening are as follows:

  - It provides relaxing breaks from more serious tasks and supports our emotional health.

  - It illustrates that people are selective listeners. You listen to what you want to hear. In a crowded room in which everyone seems to be talking, you can block out all the noise and engage in the conversation you are having with someone.

  - It doesn't require much emotional or physical effort.

How have your class notes changed during your college career?

- ***Listening for information.*** Listening for information involves the search for data or material. In the classroom, for example, the instructor usually has a strategy for guiding the class to desired goals. The instructor will probably stress several major points and use supporting evidence to prove or to reinforce them. When engaged in this type of listening, you could become so focused on recording every detail that you take copious notes with no organization. When listening for information:

- Use an outlining process to help you capture main ideas and supporting subpoints in a logical way.

- Watch the speaker as well as listen to him or her, since most speakers exhibit a set of mannerisms composed of gestures and vocal inflections to indicate the degree of importance or seriousness that they attach to portions of their presentation.

- Separate fact from fiction, comedy from seriousness, and truth from untruth.

- *Intensive listening.* When you listen to obtain information, solve problems, or persuade or dissuade (as in arguments), you are engaged in intensive listening. Intensive listening involves greater use of your analytical ability to proceed through problem-solving steps. When listening intensively:

  - Gain an understanding of the problem, recognize whatever limitations are involved, and know the implications of possible solutions.

  - Become a good summarizer.

  - Trace the development of the discussion and then move from there to your own analysis.

  - Feel free to "tailgate" on the ideas of others; creative ideas are generated in an open discussion.

How would you score yourself as an empathetic listener? How can you improve? How will empathetic listening be important in your career?

- *Empathetic listening.* **Empathy** occurs when a person attempts to share another's feelings or emotions. Counselors attempt to use empathetic listening in dealing with their clients, and good friends listen empathetically to each other. Empathy is a valuable trait developed by people skilled in interpersonal relations. When you take the time to listen to another, the courtesy is usually returned. When listening empathetically:

  - Avoid preoccupation with your own problems. Talking too much and giving strong nonverbal signals of disinterest destroy others' desire to talk.

  - Remember that total empathy can never be achieved simply because no two people are exactly alike. However, the more similar our experiences, the better the opportunity to put ourselves in the other person's shoes. Listening with empathy involves some genuine tact along with other good listening habits.

  - Whenever possible, listen in a one-to-one situation. Close friends who trust each other tend to engage in self-disclosure easily. Empathetic listening is enhanced when the participants exhibit trust and friendship.

Can empathy be carried too far? Explain.

Many people in positions of authority have developed excellent listening skills that apply to gaining information and to problem solving. However, an equal number of people have failed to develop good listening practices that work effectively in listening for feelings. An "open door" policy does not necessarily indicate an "open ear." A supervisor's poor listening habits may interfere with problem solving and reduce employee morale.

Give other examples of situations in which combined listening is required.

Frequently you may have to combine listening intensively and listening for feelings. Performance appraisal interviews, disciplinary conferences, and other sensitive discussions between supervisors and employees require listening intensively for accurate understanding of the message and listening empathetically for feelings, preconceived points of view, and background. The interviewing process also may combine the two types of listening. Job interviewers must try to determine how someone's personality, as well as skill and knowledge, will affect job performance. Whatever the situation, good listeners stay focused on their intended purpose.

your turn MISCUE

A nurse reported a severe reaction suffered by a patient due to a listening error. The patient's physician had given the nurse a verbal order via cell phone to "discontinue the I.V. for now." However, what the nurse heard was "just continue the I.V. for now." She even repeated the orders back to the doctor because the connection wasn't crystal clear; she then documented what she had heard in the patient's chart. The patient developed negative symptoms before the physician was able to see her and review her chart.[15]

- How could this communication error have been prevented?
- If the patient sued for injury, who would be at fault?
- What are the implications of using cell phones for critical conversations?

Bad Listening Habits

Physicians must first diagnose the nature of a person's medical problems before prescribing treatment. In the same way, you can't improve your listening unless you understand some of the nonphysical ailments of your own listening. Most of us have developed bad listening habits in one or more of the following areas:

- **Faking attention.** Have you ever left a classroom lecture and later realized that you had no idea what went on? Have you ever been introduced to someone only to realize 30 seconds later that you missed the name? If you had to answer "yes" to these questions, join the huge club of "fakers of attention." Isn't it amazing that we can look directly at a person, nod, smile, and pretend to be listening?

What is your own worst listening habit? What can you do to eliminate it?

- **Allowing disruptions.** Listening properly requires both physical and emotional effort. As a result, we welcome disruptions of almost any sort when we are engaged in somewhat difficult listening. The next time someone enters your classroom or meeting room, notice how almost everyone in the room turns away from the speaker and the topic to observe the latecomer.

- **Overlistening.** Overlistening occurs when listeners attempt to record in writing or in memory so many details that they miss the speaker's major points. Overlisteners "can't see the forest for the trees."

- **Stereotyping.** Most people use their prejudices and perceptions of others as a basis for developing stereotypes. As a result, we make spontaneous judgments about others based on their appearances, mannerisms, dress, speech delivery, and whatever other criteria play a role in our judgments. If a speaker doesn't meet our standards in any of these areas, we simply turn off our listening and assume the speaker can't have much to say.

The listener has an ethical responsibility to give full, unbiased attention to the speaker's verbal and nonverbal message.

- **Dismissing subjects as uninteresting.** People tend to use "uninteresting" as a rationale for not listening. Unfortunately, the decision is usually made before the topic is ever introduced. A good way to lose an instructor's respect when you have to miss class is to ask, "Are we going to do anything important in class today?"

- *Failing to observe nonverbal aids.* Good listening requires the use of eyes as well as ears. To listen effectively, you must observe the speaker. Facial expressions and body motions always accompany speech and contribute much to messages. If you do not watch the speaker, you may miss the meaning.

In addition to recognizing bad listening habits and the variety of barriers to effective listening, you must recognize that listening isn't easy. Many bad listening habits develop simply because the speed of spoken messages is far slower than our ability to receive and process them. Normal speaking speeds are between 100 and 150 words a minute. The human ear can actually distinguish words in speech in excess of 500 words a minute, and many people read at speeds well beyond 500 words a minute. Finally, our minds process thoughts at thousands of words a minute.

Because individuals can't speak fast enough to challenge our ability to listen, listeners have a responsibility to make spoken communication effective. Good listening typically requires considerable mental and emotional effort.

Suggestions for Effective Listening

Because feedback and nonverbal signs are available, you can enhance the effectiveness of your face-to-face listening by following these suggestions:

- *Minimize environmental and mental distractions.* Take time to listen. Move to a quiet area where you are not distracted by noise or other conversation. Avoid becoming so preoccupied with thoughts of other projects or what you will say next that you fail to listen.

Analyze your listener response to your instructor. How can it be maximized?

- *Get in touch with the speaker.* Maintain an open mind while attempting to understand the speaker's background, prejudices, and points of view. Listen for emotionally charged words and watch for body language, gestures, facial expressions, and eye movements as clues to the speaker's underlying feelings.

- *Use your knowledge of speakers to your advantage.* Through experience, you will begin to recognize the unique speaking and organizing traits of particular individuals. Some people seem to run on and on with details before making the point. With this speaker, you will learn to anticipate the major point but not pay much attention to details. Other speakers give conclusions first and perhaps omit support for them. In this case, you will learn to ask questions to obtain further information.

- *Let the speaker know you are actively involved.* Show genuine interest by remaining physically and mentally involved; for example, avoid daydreaming, yawning, frequently breaking eye contact, looking at your watch or papers on your desk, whispering, or allowing numerous interruptions (phone calls, etc.). Encourage the speaker to continue by providing appropriate feedback either orally or nonverbally.

- *Do not interrupt the speaker.* Try to understand the speaker's full meaning, and wait patiently for an indication that you should enter the conversation.

- *Ask reflective questions that assess understanding.* Simply restate in your own words what you think the other person has said. This paraphrasing will reinforce what you have heard and allow the speaker to correct any misunderstanding or add clarification.

- *Use probing prompts to direct the speaker.* Use probing statements or questions to help the speaker define the issue more concretely and specifically.

- *Use lag time wisely.* Listening carefully should be your primary focus; however, you can think ahead at times as well. Thinking ahead can help you develop a sense of the speaker's logic, anticipate future points, and evaluate the validity of the speaker's ideas. Making written or mental notes allows you to provide useful

Go to the text support site (www.thomsonedu.com/bcomm/lehman) and complete the listening questionnaire found at the following website: http://www.highgain.com/SELF/index.php

You may link to this URL or to www.thomsonedu.com/bcomm/lehman for updated sites from the text support site.

Send your instructor an email that summarizes your thoughts on the following:

1. How did you rate as a listener?

2. What areas did you target for improvement in your listening skills?

feedback when the opportunity arises. If you cannot take notes during the conversation, record important points as soon as possible so you can summarize the speaker's key points.

You can learn more about developing effective listening skills by completing the Case Analysis at the end of this chapter.

Group Communication

Objective 4
Identify factors affecting group and team communication.

Although much of your spoken communication in business will occur in one-to-one relationships, another frequent spoken communication activity will likely occur when you participate in groups, primarily groups within the organizational work environment. The work of groups, committees, and teams has become crucial in most organizations.

Increasing Focus on Groups

Developments among U.S. businesses in recent years have shifted attention away from the employment of traditional organizational subunits as the only mechanisms for achieving organizational goals and toward the increased use of groups.

Businesses today are streamlining their operations, often referred to as downsizing, rightsizing, *or* reengineering. *How is this process affecting organizational charts? The communication process?*

- ***Flat organizational structures.*** Many businesses today are downsizing and eliminating layers of management. Companies implementing Total Quality Management programs are reorganizing to distribute the decision-making power throughout the organization. The trend is to eliminate functional or departmental boundaries. Instead, work is reorganized in cross-disciplinary teams that perform broad core processes (e.g., product development and sales generation) and not narrow tasks (e.g., forecasting market demand for a particular product).

  In a flat organizational structure, communicating across the organization chart (among the cross-disciplinary teams) becomes more important than communicating up and down in a top-heavy hierarchy. An individual may take on an expanded **role** as important tasks are assumed. This role may involve power and authority that surpasses the individual's **status,** or formal position in the organizational chart. Much of the communication involves face-to-face meetings with team members rather than numerous, time-consuming "handoffs" as the product moves methodically from one department to another.

The time needed to design a new card at Hallmark Cards decreased significantly when the company adopted a flat organizational structure. Team members representing the former functional areas (graphic artists, writers, marketers, and others) now work in a central area, communicating openly and frequently, solving problems and making decisions about the entire process as a card is being developed. For example, a writer struggling with a verse for a new card can solicit immediate input from the graphic artist working on the team rather than finalizing the verse and then "handing it off" to the art department.[16]

- **Heightened Focus on Cooperation.** Competition has been a characteristic way of life in U.S. companies, not only externally with other businesses, but also internally. Organizations and individuals compete for a greater share of scarce resources, for a limited number of positions at the top of organizations, and for esteem in their professions. Such competition is a healthy sign of the human desire to succeed, and, in terms of economic behavior, competition is fundamental to the private enterprise system. At the same time, when excessive competition replaces the cooperation necessary for success, communication may be diminished, if not eliminated.

What places do competition and cooperation have in contemporary organizations?

  Just as you want to look good in the eyes of your coworkers and supervisors, units within organizations want to look good to one another. This attitude may cause behavior to take the competitive form, a "win/lose" philosophy. When excessive competition has a negative influence on the performance of the organization, everyone loses.

  Although competition is appropriate and desirable in many situations, many companies have taken steps through open communication and information and reward systems to reduce competition and to increase cooperation. Cooperation is more likely when the competitors (individuals or groups within an organization) have an understanding of and appreciation for others' importance and functions. This cooperative spirit is characterized as a *win/win philosophy*. One person's success is not achieved at the expense or exclusion of another. Groups identify a solution that everyone finds satisfactory and is committed to achieving. Reaching this mutual understanding requires a high degree of trust and effective interpersonal skills, particularly empathetic and intensive listening skills, and the willingness to communicate long enough to agree on an action plan that is acceptable to everyone.

Characteristics of Effective Groups

Recall a group of which you were a member. Why was the group formed? How did you achieve your group goals?

Groups form for synergistic effects; that is, through pooling their efforts, group members can achieve more collectively than they could individually. At the same time, the social nature of groups contributes to the individual goals of members. Communication in small groups leads to group decisions that are generally superior to individual decisions. The group process can motivate members, improve thinking, and assist attitude development and change. The emphasis that a particular group places on task and maintenance activities is based on several factors.

As you consider the following factors of group communication, try to visualize their relationship to the groups to which you have belonged, such as in school, religious organizations, athletics, and social activities.

- **Common goals.** In effective groups, participants share a common goal, interest, or benefit. This focus on goals allows members to overcome individual differences of opinion and to negotiate acceptable solutions.

- **Role perception.** People who are invited to join groups have perceptions of how the group should operate and what it should achieve. In addition, each member

TEAM ENVIRONMENT

has a self-concept that dictates how he or she will behave. Those known to be aggressive will attempt to be confrontational and forceful; those who like to be known as moderates will behave in moderate ways by settling arguments rather than initiating them. In successful groups, members play a variety of necessary roles and seek to eliminate nonproductive ones.

- **Longevity.** Groups formed for short-term tasks, such as arranging a dinner and program, will spend more time on the task than on maintenance. However, groups formed for long-term assignments, such as an audit of a major corporation by a team from a public accounting firm, may devote much effort to maintenance goals. Maintenance includes division of duties, scheduling, record keeping, reporting, and assessing progress.

Many prefer groups with an odd number of members.

- **Size.** The smaller the group, the more its members have the opportunity to communicate with each other. Conversely, large groups often inhibit communication because the opportunity to speak and interact is limited. When broad input is desired, large groups may be good. When extensive interaction is the goal, smaller groups may be more effective. Interestingly, large groups generally divide into smaller groups for maintenance purposes, even when the large group is task oriented. Although much research has been conducted in the area of group size, no optimal number of members has been identified. Groups of five to seven members are thought to be best for decision-making and problem-solving tasks. An odd number of members is often preferred because decisions are possible without tie votes.

How can a group experience conformity without sacrificing individual expression?

- **Status.** Some group members will appear to be better qualified than others. Consider a group in which the chief executive of the organization is a member. When the chief executive speaks, members agree. When members speak, they tend to direct their remarks to the one with high status—the chief executive. People are inclined to communicate with peers as their equals, but they tend to speak upward to their supervisor and downward to lower-level employees. In general, groups require balance in status and expertise.

- **Group norms.** A **norm** is a standard or average behavior. All groups possess norms. An instructor's behavior helps establish classroom norms. If an instructor is generally late for class, students will begin to arrive late. If the instructor permits talking during lectures, the norm will be for students to talk. People conform to norms because conformity is easy and nonconformity is difficult and uncomfortable. Conformity leads to acceptance by other group members and creates communication opportunities.

- **Leadership.** The performance of groups depends on several factors, but none is more important than leadership. Some hold the mistaken view that leaders are not necessary when an organization moves to a group concept. The role of leaders changes substantially, but they still have an important part to play. The ability of a group leader to work toward task goals while contributing to the development of group and individual goals is often critical to group success. Leadership activities may be shared among several participants, and leadership may also be rotated, formally or informally. The leader can establish norms, determine who can speak and when, encourage everyone to contribute, and provide the motivation for effective group activity.[17]

Group Roles

Which role do you view as being more destructive to group function?

Groups are made up of members who play a variety of roles, both positive and negative. Negative roles detract from the group's purposes and include the following:

- **Isolate**—one who is physically present but fails to participate
- **Dominator**—one who speaks too often and too long
- **Free rider**—one who does not do his or her fair share of the work

- *Detractor*—one who constantly criticizes and complains
- *Digresser*—one who deviates from the group's purpose
- *Airhead*—one who is never prepared
- *Socializer*—one who pursues only the social aspect of the group

Perhaps you recognize one or more of the negative roles, based on your personal group experiences. Or perhaps your group experiences have been positive as a result of members' playing positive group roles that promote the group's purposes:

- *Facilitator* (also known as *gatekeeper*)—one who makes sure everyone gets to talk and be heard
- *Harmonizer*—one who keeps tensions low
- *Record keeper*—one who maintains records of events and activities and informs members
- *Reporter*—one who assumes responsibility for preparing materials for submission
- *Leader*—one who assumes a directive role

What group roles have you played? What were the results?

In healthy groups, members may fulfill multiple roles, which rotate as the need arises. Negative roles are extinguished as the group communicates openly about its goals, strategies, and expectations. The opinions and viewpoints of all members are encouraged and expected.

From Groups to Teams

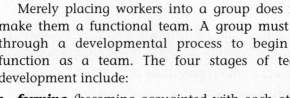

While some use the terms *group* and *team* interchangeably, others distinguish between them. The major distinction between a group and a team is in members' attitudes and level of commitment. A team is typified by a clear identity and a high level of commitment on the part of members. A variety of strategies have been used for organizing workers into teams:

- A *task force* is generally given a single goal with a limited time to achieve it.
- A *quality assurance team,* or quality circle, focuses on product or service quality, and projects can be either short- or long-term.
- A *cross-functional team* brings together employees from various departments to solve a variety of problems, such as productivity issues, contract estimations and planning, and multidepartment difficulties.
- A *product development team* concentrates on innovation and the development cycle of new products, and is usually cross-functional in nature. Recall the organizational chart illustrated in Figure 1-3. Now consider the impact of team structures, as shown in Figure 2-2.

While chain of command is still at work in formal organizational relationships and responsibilities, team structures unite people from varying portions of the organization. Work teams are typically given the authority to act on their conclusions, although the level of authority varies, depending on the organization and the purpose of the team. Typically, the group supervisor retains some responsibilities, some decisions are made completely by the team, and the rest are made jointly.

Merely placing workers into a group does not make them a functional team. A group must go through a developmental process to begin to function as a team. The four stages of team development include:

What are some reasons that a team may be unable to advance to the performing stage of team development?

- *forming* (becoming acquainted with each other and the assigned task)

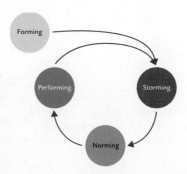

Figure 2-2

Organizational Chart with Hierarchical and Team Structures

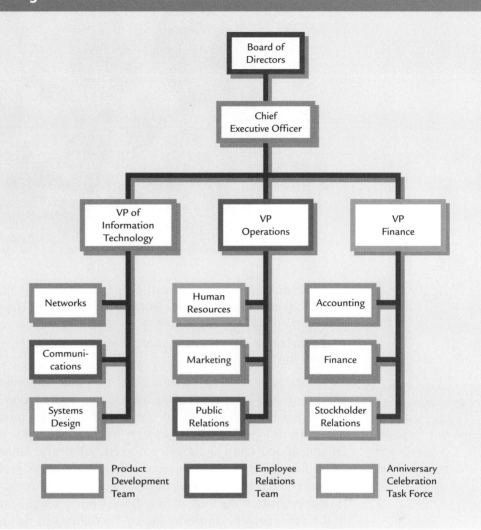

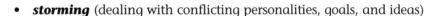

- *storming* (dealing with conflicting personalities, goals, and ideas)
- *norming* (developing strategies and activities that promote goal achievement)
- *performing* (reaching the optimal performance level).

For a variety of reasons, teams are often unable to advance through all four stages of development. Even long-term teams may never reach the optimal performing stage, settling instead for the acceptable performance of the norming stage.

Projects and activities to promote your team's successful movement through the predictable stages are provided in the *Building High-Performance Teams* handbook that accompanies this text.

Research into what makes workplace teams effective indicates that training is beneficial for participants in such areas as problem solving, goal setting, conflict resolution, risk taking, active listening, and recognizing the interests and achievement of others. Participants need to be able to satisfy one another's basic needs for belonging, personal recognition, and support. Team members at the performing stage of team development exhibit the following behaviors:[18]

- **Commitment.** They are focused on the mission, values, goals, and expectations of the team and the organization.
- **Cooperation.** They have a shared sense of purpose, mutual gain, and teamwork.

Technology can facilitate electronic meetings that allow participants in various locations to communicate as a unified group.

© Comstock/Comstock Images/Jupiter Images

- **Communication.** They know that information must flow smoothly between top management and workers. Team members are willing to face confrontation and unpleasantness when necessary.

- **Contribution.** All members share their different backgrounds, skills, and abilities with the team.

Does position on the organizational chart indicate an employee's power in the organization? Why?

Teams have existed for hundreds of years throughout many countries and cultures. Teams are more flexible than larger organizational groupings because they can be assembled, deployed, refocused, and disbanded more quickly, usually in ways that enhance rather than disrupt more permanent structures and processes. Organizational changes are often necessary, however, since support must be in place for performance evaluation, recognition, communication, and training systems. Strategies for bringing about needed change might include arranging site visits to similar organizations that already have teams, bringing a successful team to speak to the organization, and bringing in consultants to discuss the team development process.

Meeting Management

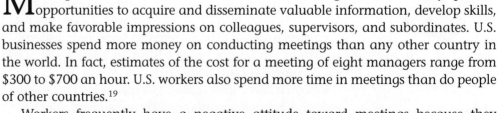

Objective 5

Discuss aspects of effective meeting management.

TEAM ENVIRONMENT

Meetings are essential for communication in organizations. They present opportunities to acquire and disseminate valuable information, develop skills, and make favorable impressions on colleagues, supervisors, and subordinates. U.S. businesses spend more money on conducting meetings than any other country in the world. In fact, estimates of the cost for a meeting of eight managers range from $300 to $700 an hour. U.S. workers also spend more time in meetings than do people of other countries.[19]

Workers frequently have a negative attitude toward meetings because they perceive they are a waste of time. Studies support this opinion, revealing that as much as one third of the time spent in meetings is unproductive. Negative attitudes toward meetings can be changed when meetings are conducted properly, giving attention to correct procedures and behavior. Successful meetings don't just happen; rather, they occur by design. Careful planning and attention to specific guidelines can help ensure the success of your meetings, whether they are conducted in a face-to-face format or electronically.

Visit the following website and take the Communications Style survey: http://www.stylesurveys.com/

Print out the information about your dominant communication style(s). Write a short summary of what the survey results reveal to you in terms of your interactions with others. What are your apparent strengths? What are your areas for improvement?

Face-to-Face Meetings

Face-to-face meetings continue to be the most-used meeting format in most organizations. They offer distinct advantages and are appropriate in the following situations:[20]

- When you need the richest nonverbal cues, including body, voice, proximity, and touch.
- When the issues are especially sensitive.
- When the participants don't know one another.
- When establishing group rapport and relationships are crucial.
- When the participants can be in the same place at the same time.

Overly dominant meeting participants can be as detrimental as the isolates who do not contribute.

Face-to-face meetings may be enhanced with the use of various media tools such as flipcharts, handouts, and electronic slide shows. While face-to-face meetings provide a rich nonverbal context and direct human contact, they also have certain limitations. In addition to the obvious logistical issues of schedules and distance, face-to-face meetings may be dominated by overly vocal, quick-to-speak, and high-status members. An additional potential obstacle to communication results from the differences in communication styles that men and women typically exhibit. The Strategic Forces feature "Communication Styles of Men and Women" describes how such problems can occur and what can be done to overcome possible difficulties in communicating.

Electronic Meetings

A variety of technologies is available to facilitate electronic meetings. Participants may communicate with one another through telephones, personal computers, or video broadcast equipment using groupware or meeting management software applications. Electronic meetings offer certain advantages. They facilitate geographically dispersed groups, because they provide the choice of meeting at different places/same time, different places/different times, same place/same time, or same place/different times. Electronic meetings also speed up meeting follow-up activities because decisions and action items may be recorded electronically.

Communication Styles of Men and Women

Research on communication patterns in mixed-gender work groups shows that the traditional behaviors of men and women may restrict the richness of discussion and limit the productivity of the group. The basic male approach to work tasks is confrontational and results oriented. By contrast, the female method of working is collaborative and oriented toward concern for individuals. The adversarial male style leads to respect, while the collaborative female style engenders rapport. Differences in male and female behavior that accentuate gender differences are often so subtle that group members may not be aware of what is happening. Here is a partial listing of those differences:

- Men are more likely to control discussion through introducing topics, interrupting, and talking more than women.

- Women not only talk less, but often assume supportive rather than leadership roles in conversation and receive less attention for their ideas from the group.

- Both men and women may expect group members to follow gender-stereotyped roles that can limit each individual's contributions (for example, always selecting a man as leader or a woman as note taker).

- Either women or men may use exclusionary language that reinforces gender stereotypes

and that others in the group find offensive.

- Women may exhibit verbal characteristics of submissiveness (allowing sentence endings to trail off or using a shrill voice), while men communicate in ways that restrict and control a group (raising the voice or ignoring ideas generated by women).

© /ImageShop/Jupiter Images

- Men's nonverbal behavior (extended eye contact, a condescending touch, or overt gestures) may convey messages of dominance, while women's nonverbal behavior (smiling, hair-twirling, or primly crossed legs) may suggest a lack of self-confidence and power.

- Men and women may sit separately, thereby limiting cross-gender interaction.

Until recently, most research on differences between the communi-

cation styles of men and women focused on face-to-face interactions. Current research has also addressed computer-mediated communication (CMC), such as email, instant messaging, and electronic meetings. Such studies indicate differences in the communication patterns of men and women. For example, women using CMC with other women develop more disclosure and sense of community, whereas men using CMC with other men seem to ignore the socio-emotional aspects of group functioning and are more likely to use mild flaming (emotional language outbursts). Overall, men are less satisfied with the CMC experience and show lower levels of group development than do women.

While caution is advised concerning stereotyping of men and women in communication situations, knowing what behaviors may limit the group process is imperative to maximizing results. Group members may need awareness training to assist in recognizing behaviors that may hinder team performance and in overcoming barriers that may limit the effectiveness of their communication. Differences can also be used to productive advantage. You will explore age-related barriers to group communication in Chapter 3.

Application

Locate an article on cross-gender communication. Compose a list of suggestions for improving cross-gender communications in the work environment. Indicate with a star those that you feel would be most helpful to you in your professional activities and that you will commit to work on as part of your self-improvement.

Electronic meetings also have certain limitations:[21]

- They cannot replace face-to-face contact, especially when group efforts are just beginning and when groups are trying to build group values, trust, and emotional ties.
- They may make it harder to reach consensus, because more ideas are generated and because it may be harder to interpret the strength of other members' commitment to their proposals.
- The success of same-time meetings is dependent on all participants having excellent keyboarding skills to engage in rapid-fire, in-depth discussion. This limitation may be overcome as voice input systems become more prevalent.

Suggestions for Effective Meetings

Whether you engage in face-to-face or electronic meetings, observing the following guidelines may help to ensure that your meetings are productive:

- *Limit meeting length and frequency.* Any meeting held for longer than an hour or more frequently than once a month should be scrutinized. Ask yourself whether the meeting is necessary. Perhaps the purpose can be achieved in another way, such as email, instant messaging, or telephone.
- *Make satisfactory arrangements.* Select a date and time convenient for the majority of expected participants. For face-to-face meetings, plan the meeting site with consideration for appropriate seating for attendees, media equipment, temperature and lighting, and necessary supplies. For electronic meetings, check hardware and software and connectivity components.
- *Distribute the agenda well in advance.* The **agenda** is a meeting outline that includes important information: date, beginning and ending time, place, and topics to be discussed and responsibilities of those involved. Having the agenda prior to the meeting allows participants to know what is expected of them. A sample agenda is provided in the *Building High-Performance Teams* handbook.
- *Encourage participation.* While it is certainly easier for one person to make decisions, the quality of the decision making is often improved by involving the team. Rational decision making may begin with **brainstorming,** the generation of many ideas from among team members. Brainstormed ideas can then be discussed and ranked, followed by some form of voting.
- *Maintain order.* An organized democratic process ensures that the will of the majority prevails, the minority is heard, and group goals are achieved as expeditiously as possible. Proper parliamentary procedure may be followed in formal meetings, as outlined in sources such as *Robert's Rules of Order* and *Jones' Parliamentary Procedure at a Glance.* For less formal meetings, a more relaxed approach may be taken to ensure that everyone has an opportunity to share in the decision making.

What is the relationship between conflict and consensus?

- *Manage conflict.* In an autocratic organization, conflict may be avoided because employees are conditioned to be submissive. Such an environment, however, leads to smoldering resentment. On the other hand, conflict is a normal part of any team effort and can lead to creative discussion and superior outcomes. Maintaining focus on issues and not personalities helps ensure that conflict is productive rather than destructive.
- *Seek consensus.* While unanimous agreement on decisions is an optimal outcome, total agreement cannot always be achieved. **Consensus** represents the collective opinion of the group, or the informal rule that all team members can live with at least 70 percent of what is agreed upon.

- *Prepare thorough minutes.* Minutes provide a concise record of meeting actions, ensure the tracking and follow-up of issues from previous meetings, and assist in the implementation of previously reached decisions. A format for meeting minutes is provided in the *Building High-Performance Teams* handbook.

eBay Redefines the International Marketplace

EBay has become a marketing phenomenon. It has empowered people to create their own businesses and has changed the way people think about junk they once might have sold at garage sales. More importantly, it has demonstrated that trust between strangers can be established over the Internet. According to eBay spokesperson Hani Durzy, "The Internet has leveled the playing field in terms of commerce, allowing individuals, small business, and big corporations to all compete against each other."[22] As it redefines consumer culture, the tremendously successful auction site stirs debate over its impact on society. Is it a portal to a new, global society? Does it elevate materialism above all other belief systems? Does it define who we are as a society?

©/AP Graphics Bank

Activities

1. Visit eBay at http://www.eBay.com. Click on the Learning Center to find out more about the overview of the company, its executive team, and current press releases.

2. Locate the following article through Business & Company Resource Center (http://bcrc. swlearning.com) or from another database available through your campus library that discusses the international challenges faced by eBay and write a brief summary of the unique communication challenges eBay has faced in dealing with customers in Germany and Korea:

   Schoenfeld, E. (2005, January–February). The world according to eBay: The online auction giant is on a spectacular international growth tear; here's Meg Whitman's master plan for global domination. *Business 2.0, 6*(1), 76(6).

3. In class or online, discuss the positive and negative impacts of eBay on commerce and society.

   http://www.ebay.com

Meetings are an important management tool and are useful for idea exchange. They also provide opportunities for you, as a meeting participant, to communicate impressions of power and status. Knowing how to present yourself and your ideas and exhibiting knowledge about correct meeting management will assist you in your career advancement.

Employees working to establish virtual teams at Dow Chemical take courses in virtual team etiquette and online meeting management. You may also visit the text support site at www.thomsonedu.com/bcomm/ lehman to learn more about maximizing the effectiveness of **virtual teams** that have members in more than one location. Other useful ideas about preparing for and conducting meetings are available at the NetMeeting website (http://www.microsoft.com/windows/ netmeeting/default.asp). The Electronic Café located at the end of Chapter 10 will provide you with additional activities and experiences designed to make you a more effective meeting participant.

©/AP Graphics Bank

Summary

1. **Explain how behavioral theories about human needs, trust and disclosure, and motivation relate to business communication.**

   Behavioral theories that address human needs, trust and disclosure, and motivation are essential aspects of interpersonal communication. The needs of all individuals to be heard, appreciated, wanted, and reinforced significantly affect their interpersonal communications.

2. **Describe the role of nonverbal messages in communication.**

   Nonverbal communication conveys a significant portion of meaning and includes metacommunications, which are wordless messages that accompany words, and kinesic communications, which are expressed through body language. The meanings of nonverbal messages are culturally derived.

3. **Identify aspects of effective listening.**

   Effective listening, which requires effort and discipline, is crucial to effective interpersonal communication and leads to career success. Various types of listening require different strategies.

4. **Identify factors affecting group and team communication.**

   Organizations are increasingly using group structures to achieve goals. Effective group communication results from shared purpose, constructive activity and behaviors, and positive role fulfillment among members. A team is a special type of group that is typified by strong commitment among members; this commitment results in behaviors that produce synergy.

5. **Discuss aspects of effective meeting management.**

   Face-to-face meetings and electronic meetings each offer certain advantages and disadvantages. Effective meeting management techniques and behaviors can enhance the success of meetings.

Chapter Review

1. What is meant by stroking? How does it affect interpersonal communication in the workplace? (Obj. 1)

2. When a manager says to the sales staff, "Let's try to make budget this year," what are some of the possible metacommunications? (Obj. 2)

3. What roles do culture and gender play in nonverbal communication? (Obj. 2)

4. How is the activity of listening impacted by the particular situation? (Obj. 3)

5. Discuss six bad listening habits. Which do you think is the biggest challenge for you personally? (Obj. 3)

6. What is a possible cause of most conflict between or among groups? (Obj. 4)

7. How are a group and a team different? (Obj. 4)

8. Discuss how a flat organizational structure affects communication. (Obj. 4)

9. What are some factors to consider in deciding whether to hold a face-to-face meeting or an electronic meeting? (Obj. 5)

10. Why are records such as agendas and minutes important to group success? (Obj. 5)

Digging Deeper

1. How can managers use Maslow's need levels, the Johari Window, and the management theories of McGregor and Hersey and Blanchard to improve communication with employees?

2. Why do some teams never reach the highest stage of team development? What can be done to overcome the obstacles to peak team performance?

Assessment

To check your understanding of the chapter, take the available online quizzes as directed by your instructor.

Activities

1. **Applying Behavioral Theories to Communication Situations (Obj. 1)**

   Considering Maslow's hierarchy of needs, the Johari Window, McGregor's Theory X and Y, and Hersey and Blanchard's situational leadership theory, select one of the theories and relate it to a personal communication experience you have had. How was communication enhanced or worsened by the events and behaviors that occurred? What were the ethical implications of the situation? Prepare a brief written summary of your analysis.

2. Understanding the Importance of Nonverbal Messages (Obj. 2)

In small groups, compose a list of nonverbal messages (gestures, facial expressions, etc.) that might be used by a businessperson, along with their meanings. What are some possible ways that each might be misinterpreted?

3. Identifying Appropriate Listening Styles (Obj. 3)

Identify a situation you have experienced that would be appropropriate for each of the following listening styles: casual listening, listening for information, intensive listening, and empathetic listening. Describe how you could maximize your listening experience in each case.

4. Identifying Deterrents to Group Success (Obj. 4)

In small groups, discuss negative group situations in which you have participated. These groups could be related to school, organizations, sports teams, performing groups, etc. Referring to the chapter information, identify reasons for each group's lack of success. Make a list of the most common problems identified in the team. Compare your list with that of other small groups in the class.

5. Analyzing a Meeting for Effective Behaviors (Obj. 5)

Attend a meeting of an organization of your choice. Compare the activities of the attended meeting with the "Suggestions for Effective Meetings" presented in the chapter. Email your instructor, describing the meeting attended and summarizing how well the meeting reflected the chapter suggestions and how it might have been more effective.

6. Assessing the Professional Value of Interpersonal and Group Communication Skills (Objs. 1–5)

Considering your career goal, select the three concepts presented in the chapter that you feel will be most important to your professional success. Write a one-page summary, justifying and explaining your selections.

Applications

Read	Think	Write	Speak	Collaborate

1. Boosting Team Effectiveness: Trend in Corporate America (Objs. 1, 4)

Locate the following article that describes the importance of teambuilding activities:

Kelley, D. (2005, August 29). Go team! Exercises boost effectiveness, synergy of staff. *The Gazette* (Colorado Springs), p. Business 1.

In a small groups, discuss the shift in corporate team building over the past 25 years and the value gained from various types of team-building activities. Brainstorm ways you believe these approaches could be used to boost the effectiveness of teams in an academic setting and the projected results. Share your ideas with the class in a short presentation.

2. Communicating Nonverbally in a Job Interview (Obj. 2)

Locate the following article through Business & Company Resource Center (http://bcrc.swlearning.com) or another database. This article gives useful suggestions for ensuring that your nonverbal behavior in a job interview makes a favorable impression:

Witcomb, M. (2005, February 28). Recruitment: Body talk that can make or break an interview. *Mortgage Strategy*, p. 56.

Expand the list of recommended nonverbal messages and their interpretations. Share your list with the class, complete with demonstrations, in an informal presentation.

Read	Think	Write	Speak	Collaborate

3. Analyzing Limitations of Electronic Communications (Objs. 2, 3, 5)

Consider a distance learning conference or course in which you have participated. How were nonverbal communication, listening, and other factors different from what you have experienced in traditional class settings? How do your experiences relate to the conducting of electronic meetings?

Read	Think	Write	Speak	Collaborate

4. Recognizing Events that Involve Metacommunication (Obj. 2)

Keep a journal over the next two to five days that records events that involve metacommunication. Describe how each incident influences the understanding of the verbal message involved.

Go to www.thomsonedu.com/bcomm/lehman for a downloadable version of this activity.

5. Maximizing the Effectiveness of Virtual Teams (Objs. 4, 5)

Visit the text support site at www.thomsonedu.com/bcomm/lehman to read about how to maximize the effectiveness of a virtual team. Consider the significance of this statement that appears in the posting: "Certain personality types are more likely to thrive in the virtual team experience." Develop a list of personality attributes that would enable a person to work effectively as part of a virtual team. In a short written or oral report, share your list, justifying your selections with facts and references.

6. **Documenting Meeting Activities (Obj. 5)**

Consult *Building High-Performance Teams* (your separate team handbook) for guidelines for preparing agendas and minutes.

Attend a meeting of an organization of your choice. Obtain a copy of the agenda, and prepare minutes of the meeting. Submit your meeting documentation to your instructor.

| Read | Think | Write | Speak | Collaborate |

7. **Locating Information on Nonverbal Communication in Other Cultures (Obj. 2)**

Locate one or more articles from library databases or the Internet that discuss nonverbal communication in various cultures. Compile a list of body language and behaviors that have different meanings among cultures. Discuss how ignorance of these differences might affect interpersonal communication.

8. **Discussing the Impact of Flat Organizational Structure on Communication (Obj. 4)**

Using an online database, locate an article about a company that has adopted a flat organizational structure. Write a brief summary emphasizing the effect this change in organizational structure has had on the communication process.

| Read | Think | Write | Speak | Collaborate |

9. **Analyzing Group and Team Experiences (Obj. 4)**

As a team, visit the website of the Institute for Performance Culture at http://teaming-up.com/. From the Free Resources menu tab, click on "Are you a True Team?" and together take the survey. Some of the items may not relate to your short-term project team but will provide you with ideas of issues faced in real-world work teams. Discuss the evaluation report produced from your survey. Send your instructor an email message, summarizing what your team survey

revealed and how you will use the information to improve your team performance.

10. **Using Instant Messaging (Chat) to Communicate (Objs. 3, 4)**

Following directions from your instructor, participate in an online chat with your class about one of the following topics: (a) how to overcome listening barriers, or (b) guidelines for effective group communication.

Case Analysis

Is Anyone Listening?

The ability to listen effectively is consistently rated as one of the most important skills necessary for success in the workplace. A survey of North American executives reveals that 80 percent believe that listening is one of the most important skills needed in the corporate environment. The same survey participants, however, also rated the skill as one of the most lacking. Effective listening is crucial to providing quality service, facilitating groups, training staff, improving teamwork, and supervising and managing for improved performance. In times of stress and change, effective listening is the cornerstone of workplace harmony, since it furthers interpersonal and intercultural understanding. Listening is more than just hearing. It is an interactive process that takes concentration and commitment.

Although listening is critical to our daily lives, it is taught and studied far less than the other three basic communication skills: reading, writing, and speaking. Overreliance on television and

computers also contributes to our listening problems. Much of the trouble we have communicating with others is because of poor listening skills. Studies show that we spend about 80 percent of our waking hours communicating, and at least 45 percent of that time listening. Most people can benefit from improving their listening skills. You can arrive at a fairly accurate assessment of your listening skills by thinking about your relationships with the people in your life—your boss, colleagues, best friends, family. If asked, what would they say about how well you listen? Do you often misunderstand assignments, or only vaguely remember what people have said to you? If so, you may need to improve your listening skills. These suggestions may assist you in your listening improvement:

- Become aware of biases and filters that keep you from listening effectively.

- Identify the aspects of listening that you need to improve upon.

- Get comfortable with silence.

- Monitor your body language, facial expressions, and other nonverbal signals that might appear negative.

- Listen between words for feelings.

- Give signals that you are listening.

- Take notes.

- Hear people out before cutting in with your reply.

- Don't begin answers with "I."
- Learn to ask nonaggressive questions.
- Understand that listening does not mean agreeing.

Listening skills can have a dramatic effect on your personal and professional success. By listening, you get listened to. Listening builds relationships and wins trust.[23]

Visit the text support site at www.thomsonedu.com/bcomm/lehman **to link to web resources related to this topic.**

Respond to one or more of the following activities, as directed by your instructor.

1. **GMAT** Tell why you are either a good or poor listener. Support your conclusion with reasons and/or evidence of one or more situations in which your listening was put to the test.

2. One of the sites you visited identified a plan for improving the listening skills of a negotiator. Prepare a similar plan for a position in your chosen career field (human resources manager, auditor, salesperson, etc.), adapting the points to fit the activities and expectations of the position.

3. Outline and implement a plan for improving your own listening skills. Your plan should include the following: (1) identification of your major listening weaknesses; (2) one or more strategies for overcoming each of the stated weaknesses; (3) activities or occasions in which you applied the corrective strategies, with dates and times; and (4) outcomes of your corrective strategies. Implement your plan for one week, or some other time period as specified by your instructor. Summarize in writing the results of your self-improvement project.

Inside View Part 1   Corporate Diversity

Harlem recently celebrated the grand opening of its first auto dealership in 40 years, thanks to the General Motors minority dealer development program. The 300,000 square-foot multi-level auto mall is expected to bring nearly 200 new jobs to Harlem, providing a big boost for the local economy. This project is one example of how smart companies recognize the importance of serving the needs of their important minority customer base and the commitment to diverse markets. Diversity within a company also can pay off, as Henry Ford showed many years ago when he pioneered equal pay for black workers. How can companies benefit by focusing on diversity?

 View the Part I "Corporate Diversity" video segment online at http://www. thomsonedu.com/bcomm/lehman to learn more about this issue.

How can encouraging minority enterprise development benefit a company's diversity efforts? Companies that invest their resources in minorities are supporting a very important segment of the population and may realize tremendous sales potential from diverse markets.

Reflect:

1. How is diversity good for a company?

2. How can diversity among employees within a company help that company do a better job in the marketplace?

3. What are some possible differences between an effective company diversity program and a company's public relations efforts related to diversity?

4. Why would more than 60 companies write to the Supreme Court supporting the right for a university to consider race as a factor for admission? How do you think businesses will benefit from minority college graduates in the long run?

React:

Locate the following article that contains an interview with former Kodak chairman, Daniel A. Carp about the link between diversity in the workplace and universities. He believes, as do other CEOs, that higher education is doing a poor job producing students who are comfortable in the diverse settings of today's business environment:

> D.A. Carp. (2006, January 26). A Kodak moment: former chairman Daniel A. Carp makes the case for collegiate and corporate diversity. *Diverse Issues in Higher Education, 22*(25), 28(2).

Identify ways that companies depend on universities for qualified minority employees. What difficulties occur when the pool of talented graduates is small and homogenous? Give a brief presentation on this article with your recommendations for solving the problem.

Part 2 Communication Analysis

Planning Spoken and Written Messages 3

Preparing Spoken and Written Messages 4

Chapter 3
Planning Spoken and Written Messages

Objectives

When you have completed Chapter 3, you will be able to:

1 Identify the purpose of the message and the appropriate channel.

2 Develop clear perceptions of the audience to enhance the impact of the communication and human relations.

3 Apply techniques for adapting messages to the audience, including strategies for communicating ethically and responsibly.

4 Recognize the importance of organizing a message before writing the first draft.

5 Select the appropriate message outline (deductive or inductive) for developing messages to achieve the desired response.

© Susan Van Etten

Hallmark Crafts Messages for Changing Consumer Market

Nationwide, American consumers spend about $7.5 billion a year on greeting cards.[1] Greeting cards can be a meaningful communication tool for customers, coworkers, and important business contacts and can provide a memorable, cost-effective way to build loyalty and increase customer retention. Hallmark Cards, Inc., located in Kansas City, Missouri, has been helping people say the right things at the right time for nearly 100 years, and the continued success of its cards is directly tied to effective analysis of an ever-changing audience.

 *We're not filling all the needs that people have when it comes to their relationships, but we have their 'permission' and opportunities to do so."*

As American society has become increasingly heterogeneous, Hallmark product offerings have also become more diverse. Realizing that Hispanics currently account for 11 percent of the U.S. population, the company has extended the appeal of its cards to Hispanics through its Sinceramente Hallmark line, which includes more than 2,500 Spanish-language cards. Hallmark targets its African-American consumers with its Mahogany line. The Tree of Life series, meanwhile, is aimed at Jewish customers, and in 2003, Hallmark began carrying Diwali and Eid al-Fitr cards to appeal to its Muslim clientele. Expansion into international markets has shown Hallmark that message appeal is largely influenced by cultural values. The Dutch audience, for instance, tends to be more direct than Americans, while British consumers are more reserved and less direct.

Shifting cultural demographics is only one challenge faced by Hallmark. Referring to recent internal research, Hallmark's CEO Donald J. Hall, Jr. says, "We're not filling all the needs that people have when it comes to their relationships, but we have their 'permission' and opportunities to do so."[2] Generational changes, such as the tendency of baby boomers to purchase fewer cards than their parents, and the current popularity of e-cards have given rise to the design of new products to entice consumers to card shop more often. Because women buy 80 percent of all greeting cards, Hallmark works to attract today's women, particularly those older than 45 who no longer have children at home. The Shoebox and Fresh Ink lines are designed to provide offbeat and entertaining options for those who prefer an alternative to traditional sentiments. The 9/11 tragedy and the war against terrorism also revived patriotic feelings in many people, giving rise to Hallmark products that encompass patriotic sentiments.

Hallmark knows that building good communication with friends and family, as well as customers and business partners, means that it must design text and visual messages that effectively convey intended meanings and emotions. The company must accurately visualize its ever-changing audience in order to design appealing greeting cards. You, too, will need skills in audience analysis to communicate effectively in your profession. In this chapter you will learn various analysis skills for developing effective spoken and written messages that achieve your desired purpose.

http://www.hallmark.com

SEE SHOWCASE PART 2, ON PAGE 90, FOR SPOTLIGHT COMMUNICATOR DEAN RODENBOUGH, DIRECTOR OF CORPORATE COMMUNICATIONS AT HALLMARK CARDS.

In a report entitled "Writing: A Ticket to Work . . . or a Ticket Out," the National Commission on Writing reported that two thirds of salaried employees in large companies have some writing responsibilities, and getting hired and promoted in many industries demands this skill. Writing is important; however, the Commission also concluded that one third of employees in corporate America writes poorly. Knowing that effective communication is tied to the corporate bottom line and many employees can't write well, businesses are investing $3.1 billion annually to train employees to write.[3] Remedies are needed to prevent confusion, waste, errors, lost productivity, and damaged corporate image—all caused by employees and customers and clients muddling their way through unreadable messages.

As a capable communicator, you can immediately add value to your organization and set yourself apart from your peers who are struggling to articulate ideas in writing and presentations. Communication that commands attention and can be understood easily is essential for survival in today's information explosion. As an effective communicator, you will be expected to process volumes of available information and shape useful messages that respond to the needs of customers or clients, coworkers and supervisors, and other key business partners. Additionally, increased use of electronic communication (faxes, emails, instant messages, videoconferencing, etc.) will require you to be technologically savvy and capable of adapting the rules of good communication to the demands of emerging technology.

How can you learn to plan and prepare powerful business messages? The systematic analysis process as outlined in Figure 3-1 will help you develop messages that save you and your organization valuable time and money and portray you as a capable, energetic professional. A thorough analysis of the audience and your specific communication assignment will empower you to write a first draft efficiently and to revise and proofread your message for accuracy, conciseness, and appropriate tone. You will focus on the planning process in this chapter, and then learn to prepare the message in Chapter 4.

Step 1: Determining the Purpose and Channel

Objective 1
Identify the purpose of the message and the appropriate channel.

If you are to speak or write effectively, you first must think through what you are trying to say and understand it thoroughly before you begin. Ask yourself why you are preparing the message and what you hope to accomplish. Is the purpose to get information, to answer a question, to accept an offer, to deny a request, to seek support for a product or idea? Condense the answers into a brief sentence that is the purpose for writing or the central idea of your message. You will use the central idea to organize your message to achieve the results you desire.

The major purpose of many business messages is to have the receiver understand logical information. Informative messages are used to convey the vast amounts of information needed to complete the day-to-day operations of the business—explain instructions to employees, announce meetings and procedures, acknowledge orders, accept contracts for services, and so forth. Some messages are intended to persuade—to influence or change the attitudes or actions of the receiver. These messages include promoting a product or service and seeking support for ideas and worthy causes presented to supervisors, employees, stockholders, customers/clients, and others. You will learn to prepare messages for each of these purposes.

With your purpose in mind, you can now select an appropriate channel that will increase the likelihood that the receiver will understand and accept your message.

It has been said that all business messages have some persuasive intent. Do you agree or disagree?

Identify the appropriate channel for (a) telling a customer damaged merchandise will be replaced, (b) notifying a sales rep of job termination, or (c) informing employees of a new Internet usage policy.

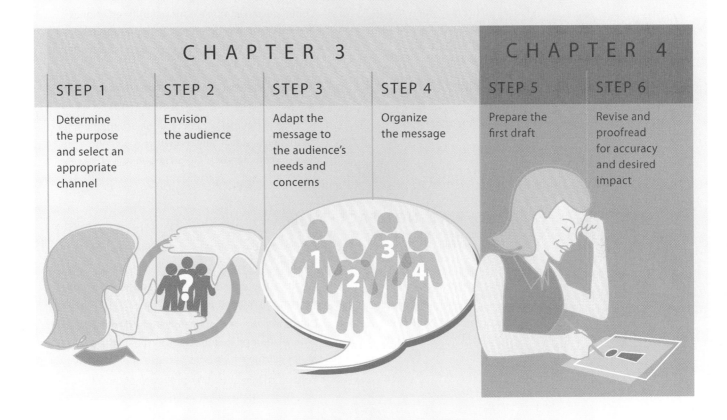

Recall the varying degree of efficiency and effectiveness of each of the typical communication channels discussed in Chapter 1. Follow the guidelines in Figure 3-2 for selecting a communication channel that is most appropriate depending on the nature and location of the audience, formality and content of the message, and the need for feedback, written record, and privacy.

Step 2: Envisioning the Audience

Objective 2
Develop clear perceptions of the audience to enhance the impact of the communication and human relations.

Perception is the part of the communication process that involves how we look at others and the world around us. It's a natural tendency to perceive situations from our own limited viewpoint. We use the context of the situation and our five senses to absorb and interpret the information bombarding us in unique ways.

Individual differences in perception account for the varied and sometimes conflicting reports given by eyewitnesses to the same accident. A popular television series focuses on Monk, the "defective" detective who can see things that scores of trained police workers cannot see although they've all been looking at the same

Figure 3-2

CHANNEL	RECOMMENDED USE

TWO-WAY, FACE-TO-FACE

Person conversation	Communicate an unpleasant or highly emotional message that may be subject to misinterpretation, a persuasive message, follow-up to a complex written message, or a personal message.
Traditional group meeting	Provide an optimal communication environment for discussing and reaching consensus on critical issues.
Video or teleconference	Provide an optimal communication environment for discussing and reaching a consensus on critical issues when members are geographically dispersed.

TWO-WAY, NOT FACE-TO-FACE

Telephone call	Deliver or obtain pleasant or routine information instantly.
Voice mail message	Leave message the receiver can reply to when convenient, eliminating telephone tag.
Electronic mail or instant messaging	Deliver the same message to a large, dispersed audience; inappropriate for personal, confidential, for highly sensitive messages because of privacy issues.
	Contact colleagues while on the telephone or provide or seek general information.

ONE-WAY, NOT FACE-TO-FACE

Letter or memorandum	Deliver written record of information internally or externally.
Report or proposal	Provide a written record of procedures or policy.
Web page or blog	Communicate complex lengthy information.
Text messaging	Engage in a free-flowing dialog that ensures timely distribution and capture of knowledge about a topic of interest.
	Give immediate access to short, important messages that can be retrieved discreetly between events or detailed information that can be sent more accurately and easily than by voice mail.

crime scene. Illusions can help us understand how our senses can be tricked when there is a difference in what we expect and what really is happening. Search the Internet for optical illusions. How does your perception affect your ability to interpret the image accurately or completely?

Perception of reality is also limited by previous experiences and our attitudes toward the sender of the message. We filter messages through our own frames of reference and tend to only see things that we want to see. We support ideas that are in line with our own and decide whether to focus on the positive or the negative of a situation. We may simply refuse to hear a message that doesn't fit into our view of the world.

Much of the confusion in communication is caused by differences in the sender's and receiver's perceptions. For example, team members may clash when some members perceive the task to be of greater importance than do other people involved in the work. Perceptions vary between individuals with similar backgrounds, and even more so when people from different cultures, generations, and genders communicate. You'll explore these communication challenges in later Strategic Forces features.

Overcoming perceptual barriers is difficult but essential if you are to craft messages that meet the needs and concerns of your audience. To help you envision the audience, first focus on relevant information you know about the receiver. The more familiar you are with the receiver, the easier this task will be. When communicating with an individual, you immediately recall a clear picture of the receiver—his or her physical appearance, background (education, occupation, religion, culture), values, opinions, preferences, and so on. Most importantly, your knowledge of the receiver's reaction in similar, previous experiences will aid you in anticipating how this receiver is likely to react in the current situation. Consider the following audience characteristics:

- **Age.** A message answering an elementary-school student's request for information from your company would not be worded the same as a message answering a similar request from an adult.

- **Economic level.** A banker's collection letter to a customer who pays promptly is not likely to be the same form letter sent to clients who have fallen behind on their payments for small loans.

- **Educational/occupational background.** The technical jargon and acronyms used in a financial proposal sent to bank loan officers may be inappropriate in a proposal sent to a group of private investors.

- **Needs and concerns of the receiver.** Just as successful sales personnel begin by identifying the needs of the prospective buyer, an effective manager attempts to understand the receiver's frame of reference as a basis for organizing the message and developing the content.

- **Culture.** The vast cultural differences between people (language, expressions, customs, values, religions) increase the complexity of the communication process. An email containing typical American expressions (e.g., "The proposal was *shot down*," "projections are *on par*," and "*the competition is backed to the wall*") would likely confuse a manager from a different culture. Differences in values influence communication styles and message patterns. For example, Japanese readers value the beauty and flow of words and prefer an indirect writing approach, unlike Americans who prefer clarity and conciseness.[4] The Case Analysis allows you to explore one of the greatest

©/AP Graphics Bank

What is your favorite visual illusion? Why?

Differences in perception create challenges for effective communication.

What other information about your receiver might help to shape your message?

challenges related to international commerce—the ability to prepare clear, accurate translations into numerous languages.

- **Rapport.** A sensitive message written to a long-time client may differ significantly from a message written to a newly acquired client. The rapport created by previous dealings with the client aids understanding in a current situation.

- **Expectations.** Because accountants, lawyers, and other professionals are expected to meet high standards, a message from one of them containing errors in grammar or spelling would likely cause a receiver to question the credibility of the source.

You may find that envisioning an audience you know well is often such a conscious action that you may not even recognize that you are doing it. On the other hand, envisioning those you do not know well requires additional effort. In these cases, simply assume an empathetic attitude toward the receiver to assist you in identifying his or her frame of reference (knowledge, feelings, emotions). In other words, project mentally how you believe you would feel or react in a similar situation and use that information to communicate understanding back to the person.

Consider the use (or lack) of empathy in the following workplace examples:

Empathy is the ability to identify another's frame of reference and to communicate understanding back to the person.

In communicating with someone of another culture, how can we effectively focus on similarities while being aware of differences?

Sample Message	Problem Analysis
Example 1: A U.S. manager's instructions to a new employee from an Asian culture: "Please get to work right away inputting the financial data for the Collier proposal. Oh, I need you to get this work out ASAP. Because this proposal is just a draft, just plan to give me a quick-and-dirty job. You can clean it up after we massage the stats and get final blessings from the top dog. Do you have any questions?"	• *The use of acronyms and expressions peculiar to the U.S. environment confuse and intimidate.* • *Final open-ended question indicates the writer does not understand the importance of saving face to a person from an Asian culture. Deep cultural influences may prevent this employee from asking questions that might indicate lack of understanding.*
Example 2: An excerpt from a letter sent to Mr. Sandy Everret: Dear <u>Ms. Everett:</u> The wireless iPod kit that you expressed an interest in is now available in at your local car dealer. This innovative Bluetooth technology can be demonstrated at <u>you convience</u>. Please call your local sales representative to schedule a appointment. I remain <u>Respectfully yours,</u> Dana Merrill Dana Merrill, Manager	• *Misspelling the receiver's name (and misinterpreting the gender) and overlooking mechanical errors imply incompetence or carelessness and disrespect for the receiver.* • *The outdated closing and omission of contact information reduce the writer's credibility and show lack of genuine concern for meeting the sender's needs.*

Taking the time and effort to obtain a strong mental picture of your audience through firsthand knowledge or your empathetic attitude *before* you write will enhance your message in the following ways:

1. **Establishes rapport and credibility needed to build long-lasting personal and business relationships.** Your receivers will appreciate your attempt to connect

and understand their feelings. A likely outcome is mutual trust, which can greatly improve communication and people's feelings about you, your ideas, and themselves (as shown in the discussion of the Johari Window in Chapter 2).

2. **Permits you to address the receiver's needs and concerns.** This knowledge allows you to select relevant content and to communicate in a suitable style.

3. **Simplifies the task of organizing your message.** From your knowledge of yourself and from your experiences with others, you can predict (with reasonable accuracy) receivers' reactions to various types of messages. To illustrate, ask yourself these questions:

- Would I react favorably to a message saying my request is being granted or that a new client is genuinely pleased with a job I'd just completed?

- Would I experience a feeling of disappointment when I learn that my request has been refused or that my promised pay raise is being postponed?

- Would I need compelling arguments to convince me to purchase a new product or support a new company policy or an employer's latest suggestion for improvement?

Now, reread the questions as though you were the message recipient. Because you know *your* answers, you can predict *others'* answers with some degree of accuracy. Such predictions are possible because of commonality in human behavior.

Your commitment to identifying the needs and concerns of your audience before you communicate is invaluable in today's workplace. Organizations must focus on providing quality customer service and developing work environments supportive of talented, diverse workers. Alienating valuable customers and talented employees as a result of poor audience analysis is not an option in today's competitive environment. Empathy is also central to handling the challenges of communicating across the generations, as you'll learn in the accompanying Strategic Forces feature, "Bridging the Generation Gap."

Step 3: Adapting the Message to the Audience

Objective 3
Apply techniques for adapting messages to the audience, including strategies for communicating ethically and responsibly.

After you have envisioned your audience, you are ready to adapt your message to fit the specific needs of your audience. Adaptations include focusing on the receiver's point of view; communicating ethically and responsibly; building and protecting goodwill; using simple, contemporary language; writing concisely; and projecting a positive, tactful tone.

Focus on the Receiver's Point of View

Ideas are more interesting and appealing if they are expressed from the receiver's viewpoint. Developing a "you attitude" rather than a "me attitude" involves thinking in terms of the other person's interests and trying to see a problem from the other's point of view. A letter, memo, email, or phone call reflecting a "you attitude" sends a direct signal of sincere concern for the receiver's needs and interest.

The use of the word *you* (appropriately used) conveys to receivers a feeling that messages are specifically for them. However, if the first-person pronoun *I* is used frequently, especially as the subject, the sender may impress others as being

Bridging the Generation Gap

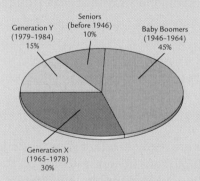

Age diversity is a reality in the United States workforce today, and the span of age continues to increase as older workers choose to work longer or re-enter the job market after retirement and as increasing numbers of younger workers enter the workplace. Companies committed to innovative team-based systems face the challenge of fostering teamwork between four generations spanning more than 60 years. The four generations working side by side include the following in the proportions shown in the accompanying figure.[5]

Figure: Pie chart showing generations:
- Generation Y (1979–1984) 15%
- Seniors (before 1946) 10%
- Baby Boomers (1946–1964) 45%
- Generation X (1965–1978) 30%

• **Matures or seniors.**

Americans over 60 years of age whose survival of hard times caused them to value hard work, sacrifice, and a strong sense of right and wrong. They like the idea of re-entering the job market after retirement or remaining there for the long haul.

• **Baby boomers.**

Set squarely in middle age, they are referred to as the "Me" generation because they grew up in boom times and were indulged and encouraged by their parents to believe their opportunities were limitless. They will work longer than their parents because of greater financial strain and a limited retirement budget.

• **Generation Xers.**

Members of the generation of the "latchkey" kid are fiercely independent, self-directed, and resourceful, but skeptical of authority and institutions because

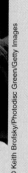

© Keith Brofsky/Photodisc Green/Getty Images

they entered the workforce in a time of downsizing and cutbacks.

• **Millennials (also called Generation Yers).**

The children and grandchildren of the boomers' children, who are the "young folks" of the workforce, are technologically savvy, active, and visually oriented due to their lifetime experience in a high-tech world.

Studies indicate that generational conflict is often unfounded. For instance, baby boomer resistance to Generation X is based on an incorrect assumption that Gen Xers are slackers. Experience, however, has confirmed more positive characteristics. Older workers should show trust for young workers and give them freedom to demonstrate their talents. Respectively, younger workers might seek to learn from older workers and ask for coaching and mentoring.

Misconceptions such as these can cause unwarranted resistance. When properly managed, companies with a strong mix of older and younger workers have a distinct competitive edge. Each generation has something to offer; younger workers bring new ideas; older workers bring experience. Getting these workers to work together effectively requires effective communication, beginning with an appreciation for the value of diversity. Visit the text support site at www.thomsonedu.com/bcomm/lehman to learn about ways to avoid clashes between the generations.

Application

1. *Interview a person from a generation other than your own. Assist him/her in identifying the generation to which he/she belongs. Include the following questions in your interview:*

   • Considering your own experiences with supervisors and coworkers, what type of management styles and communication patterns do you find to be most effective?

   • What guidelines can you offer to managers of older (or younger) generations for successfully communicating with persons of your generation?

2. *Based on interview information and your own readings, develop a list of organizational guidelines for communicating most effectively with persons from the interviewee's generation.*

Reword the following to show more you attitude: "I'm asking all work teams to generate a list of innovative product ideas."

self-centered—always talking about self. Compare the following examples of sender-centered and receiver-centered statements:

I- or Sender-Centered	Receiver-Centered
<u>I</u> want to take this opportunity to offer <u>my</u> congratulations on your recent promotion to regional manager.	Congratulations on your recent promotion to regional manager.
<u>We</u> allow a 2 percent discount to customers who pay their total invoices within 10 days.	Customers who pay within 10 days may deduct 2 percent from their total invoice. (*You* could be the subject in a message to a customer.)
<u>I</u> am interested in ordering . . .	Please send me . . . (*You* is the understood subject.)

Compliments (words of deserved praise) are another effective way of increasing a receiver's receptiveness to ideas that follow. Give sincere compliments judiciously as they can do more harm than good if paid at the wrong time, in the wrong setting, in the presence of the wrong people, or for the wrong reasons. Likewise, avoid flattery (words of undeserved praise). Although the recipient may accept your flattery as a sincere compliment, chances are the recipient will interpret your undeserved praise as an attempt to seek to gain favor or special attention. Suspicion of your motive makes effective communication less likely.

To cultivate a "you attitude," concentrate on the following questions:

- Does the message address the receiver's major needs and concerns?

- Would the receiver feel this message is receiver-centered? Is the receiver kept clearly in the picture?

- Will the receiver perceive the ideas to be fair, logical, and ethical?

- Are ideas expressed clearly and concisely (to avoid lost time, money, and possible embarrassment caused when messages are misunderstood)?

- Does the message promote positive business relationships—even when the message is negative? For example, are *please, thank you,* and other courtesies used when appropriate? Are ideas stated tactfully and positively and in a manner that preserves the receiver's self-worth and cultivates future business?

- Is the message sent promptly to indicate courtesy?

- Does the message reflect the high standards of a business professional: quality paper, accurate formatting, quality printing, and absence of misspellings and grammatical errors?

Word choice is vital!

Responding to a stock analyst's negative comments about Showbiz's stock price, Chuck E. Cheese, the company's large rodent icon, crafted a lighthearted response focusing on the company's fun-loving slogan, "Where a Kid Can Be a Kid!" Read Chuck E.'s letter available at the text support site (www.thomsonedu.com/bcomm/lehman) and consider how the tone of the letter affected the overall impact of the message and the company's public relations efforts.

LEGAL & ETHICAL CONSTRAINTS

Concentrating on these points will boost the receiver's confidence in the sender's competence and will communicate nonverbally that the receiver is valued enough to merit your best effort. For people who practice courtesy and consideration, the "you attitude" is easy to incorporate into written and spoken messages.

Communicate Ethically and Responsibly

Were you ever the recipient of an unethical business practice? Describe the incident, your feelings, and the outcome.

The familiar directive "with power comes responsibility" applies especially to your use of communication skills. Because business communication affects the lives of many, you must accept responsibility for using it to uphold your own personal values and your company's standards of ethical conduct. Before speaking or writing, use the following guidelines to help you communicate ethically and responsibly.

In small groups, discuss the ethics of inflating a résumé to increase the chances of getting a job interview.

- ***Is the information stated as truthfully, honestly, and fairly as possible?*** Good communicators recognize that ensuring a free flow of essential information is in the interest of the public and the organization. The Spotlight Communicator from Hallmark shares the positive effect open, timely internal communication has had on the company's financial performance and its relationship with employees. On the other hand, Merck, the manufacturer of the prescription pain reliever Vioxx, was sued by thousands of patients and patients' families for withholding information about known heart risks associated with taking the drug.[6] Your honor, honesty, and credibility will build strong, long-lasting relationships and lead to the long-term success of your company. Sending complete, accurate, and timely information regardless of whether it supports your views will help you build that credibility.

- ***Does the message embellish or exaggerate the facts?*** Legal guidelines related to advertising provide clear guidance for avoiding *fraud*, the misrepresentation of products or services; however, overzealous sales representatives or imaginative writers can use language skillfully to create less-than-accurate perceptions in the minds of readers. Businesses have learned the hard way that overstating the capabilities of a product or service (promising more than can be delivered) is not good for business in the long run. Researchers are at times tempted to overstate their findings to ensure continued funding or greater publicity. Eric T. Peohlman,

Translation Challenges

When traveling abroad, Americans expect—and in fact depend on—the people in the countries they visit to speak English. Often much gets mangled in the translations. In Budapest, Hungary, for example, a sign outside a hotel elevator reports: "The lift is being fixed for the next day. During that time we regret that you will be unbearable." A Bangkok, Thailand, dry cleaning establishment urges customers to "drop your trousers here for best results."[7] While humorous, such butchered translations betray a serious problem: The United States remains dependent on others knowing the English language. We are linguistically underdeveloped when compared to other nations.

- **Read about the need for over-the-phone interpreters.** Access the Business & Company Resource Center at http://bcrc.swlearning.com or another database available from your campus library to read about how insurance companies meet the translation needs of their diverse clientele. Search for the following article that is available in full text:

  Chordas, L. (2005, February). Ending the global disconnect: Over-the-phone interpreters help insurers bridge the gap. Best's Review, 105(10), 88.

  Write a 100-word abstract of the article, reflecting the important ideas presented.

- **Practice your translation from English to Spanish.** Visit www.thomsonedu.com/bcomm/lehman to explore the translation of English to Spanish. Refer to Chapter 3's Electronic Café that links you to a website that translates words from English to Spanish,

revealing the translation in print and audibly. Use the tool to translate a passage that your instructor will provide.

- **Explore language translation.** Go to your online course; your instructor will have translated it into a language other than English. Visit the following website that will assist you in determining what language your online course is now in: http://www.xrce.xerox.com/competencies/content-analysis/tools/guesser

  Once you have determined the language in use, email your instructor with the answer.

- **Experience language and culture.** Access your text support site (www.thomsonedu.com/bcomm/lehman) for a translation tool that allows you to hear and read vocabulary from a number of languages and to gain knowledge about the cultures of various countries.

a medical researcher, acknowledged that while at the University of Vermont he fabricated data in 17 applications for federal grants to make his work seem more promising. Under a plea agreement, he was barred for life from receiving federal funding and had to pay back $180,000, as well as asking scientific journals to retract and corrrect 10 articles he had authored.[8] Developing skill in communicating persuasively will be important throughout your profession. The techniques you will read about in this text, such as those related to writing a winning résumé and application letter, will be helpful as you begin your career; however, these techniques should *not* be used if your motive is to exploit the receiver.

- **Are the ideas expressed clearly and understandably?** If a message is to be classified as honest, you must be reasonably confident that the receiver can understand the message accurately. Ethical communicators select words that convey the exact meaning intended and that are within the reader's vocabulary.

Former top accountant at Enron Corp., Richard Causey, pleaded guilty in 2005 to securities fraud and currently serves a prison term. He admitted that he and other senior Enron managers made various false public filings and statements.[9]

Consider a plumber's frustration with the following message from the Bureau of Standards: "The effect of HCL is incompatible with the metallic piping" and "We cannot assume responsibility for the production of toxic and noxious residues with HCL." Finally the Bureau sent a message the plumber could understand: "Don't use HCL. It eats the heck out of pipes!"[10] To protect consumers, some states have passed "Plain English" laws that require certain businesses and agencies to write policies, warranties, and contracts in language an average reader can understand. You can learn more about the importance of Plain English laws by completing the Case Analysis in Chapter 4.

How bound is a business professional to "tell the truth, the whole truth, and nothing but the truth"?

- ***Is your viewpoint supported with objective facts?*** Are facts accurately documented to allow the reader to judge the credibility of the source and to give credit where credit is due? Can opinions be clearly distinguished from facts? Have you evaluated honestly any real or perceived conflict of interest that could prevent you from preparing an unbiased message? You will learn to develop objective, well-documented written reports and presentations in Chapters 9–12.

- ***Are ideas stated with tact and consideration that preserves the receiver's self-worth?*** The metaphor, "An arrow, once it is shot, cannot be recalled," is used to describe the irrevocable damage caused by cruel or unkind words.[11] Ego-destroying criticism, excessive anger, sarcasm, hurtful nicknames, betrayed secrets, rumors, and malicious gossip pose serious ethical problems in the workplace because they can ruin reputations, humiliate, and damage a person's self-worth. Serious legal issues arise when negative statements are false, constituting defamation. Written defamatory remarks are referred to as **libel,** and similar spoken remarks are referred to as **slander.** If you choose to make negative statements about a person, be sure the facts in question are supported. Additionally, you'll hone your abilities to convey negative information and to handle sensitive situations in a constructive, timely manner rather than ignoring them until they get out of control. For considerate, fair, and civilized use of words, follow this simple rule: Communicate with and about others with the same kindness and fairness that you wish others to use when communicating with you.

- ***Are graphics carefully designed to avoid distorting facts and relationships?*** Communicating ethically involves reporting data as clearly and accurately as possible. Misleading graphics result either from the developers' deliberate attempt to confuse the audience or from their lack of expertise in constructing ethical graphics. You will study the principles of creating graphics that show information accurately and honestly in a Strategic Forces feature in Chapter 10.

The use of profanity in the workplace can be seen not only as insensitive and offensive; it can also be interpreted as creating a hostile work environment, a legal offense, and eroding the civility of society. New York City reporter Arthur Chi'en was fired from his job as a WCBS-TV reporter for shouting profanities at hecklers. Thinking he was off the air following the completion of his report, he used strong language while the camera was still rolling. Although he apologized for his action the station terminated him, citing the recent crackdown on obscenity by the Federal Communications Commission.[12]

- What constitutes profanity?
- How have societal ideas changed concerning the use of profanity?
- How would your workplace likely respond to the use of profanity?

Build and Protect Goodwill

Goodwill arises when a business is worth more than its tangible assets. Things such as a good name and reputation, a desirable location, a unique product, and excellent customer service, can assure earnings, and so the business has more value than simply its tangible assets. Businesses go to great lengths to build and protect goodwill and thus their future. It is no surprise that effective communication is a key strategy.

Insensitive messages—whether directed to customers, employees, or business partners—can offend and alienate and will diminish a company's goodwill. Most of us don't intend to be insensitive but simply may not think carefully about the impact the tone of our words may have on others. **Tone** is the way a statement sounds and conveys the writer's or speaker's attitude toward the message and the receiver. To build and protect your company's goodwill, eliminate words that are overly euphemistic, condescending, demeaning, and biased.

Use Euphemisms Cautiously

In groups, identify two more euphemisms you have heard recently. Do you believe their use is acceptable?

A **euphemism** is a kind word substituted for one that may offend or suggest something unpleasant. For example, the idea of picking up neighborhood garbage does not sound especially inviting. Someone who does such work is often referred to as a *sanitation worker*. This term has a more pleasant connotation than *garbage collector*.

Choose the euphemistic terms rather than the negative terms shown in the following examples:

Negative Tone	Euphemistic Tone
aged or elderly	senior citizen
died	passed away
corpse in coffin	body in casket
used or secondhand	pre-owned
garbage dump	sanitary landfill
disabled/handicapped	physically challenged

Using euphemisms that ridicule or mislead the recipient can undermine your trust and credibility.

Generally, you can recognize such expressions for what they are—unpleasant ideas presented with a little sugar coating. Knowing the sender was simply trying to be polite and positive, you are more likely to react favorably. Yet you should avoid euphemisms that excessively sugarcoat and those that appear to be deliberate sarcasm. For example, to refer to a janitor as a *maintenance engineer* is to risk conveying a negative metacommunication, such as "This person does not hold a very respectable position, but I did the best I could to make it sound good." To the receiver (and to the janitor), just plain *janitor* would sound better.

You will also want to avoid **doublespeak,** or **corporate speak,** terms used to refer to euphemisms that deliberately mislead, hide, or evade the truth. This distortion of the truth is often found in military, political, and corporate language. A loss of credibility and respect results when a politician talks of "revenue enhancements" rather than "tax increases," a police officer refers to "nontraditional organized crime" rather than gang activity, or a military spokesperson speaks of "collateral damage" or "friendly fire" rather than civilians killed accidentally by the military's own weapons. Companies use doublespeak when they make "workforce reductions" or offer workers a "career opportunity adjustment" or "voluntary termination." One company called the permanent shutdown of a steel plant an "indefinite idling" in an attempt to avoid paying severance or pension benefits to the displaced workers.[13]

The most horrible example of business doublespeak occurred in a paragraph-long memo that was thrown aside because the standard buzzwords filling the memo led the manager to believe it was unimportant. The memo, sent to the engineering operating staff at the nuclear power plant at Three Mile Island two weeks before a major accident, warned of exactly the things that went wrong. The cost of doublespeak in this internal communication is estimated at about $3 billion annually.[14]

How can you ensure quality in a collaboratively written document? Perhaps someone makes unnecessary additions or makes ill-advised edits such as revising to make the document "sound more professional" while sacrificing clarity. What can you do?

Despite your training in writing, you may fall in the trap of mirroring the writing of people above you on the career ladder who prefer writing in doublespeak. They choose doublespeak over clear, concise writing because of the misguided belief that doublespeak makes them sound informed and professional. Such vagueness protects them when they're unsure how their messages will be received and makes writing easy once they learn the code. Instead of falling into doublespeak, learn to develop clear, concise messages that clarify ideas and provide direction to recipients regardless of their culture while enhancing your credibility as an honest communicator. A CEO of a writing training company has another interesting angle on clear writing. He contends that "articulation of thought is an element of intelligence, and you can increase your intelligence through writing." Working to articulate ideas clearly and logically through writing makes people smarter![15] That is a motivating reason for perfecting writing (and speaking) skills in our professional and personal lives.

Avoid Condescending or Demeaning Expressions

Condescending words seem to imply that the communicator is temporarily coming down from a level of superiority to join the receiver on a level of inferiority; such words damage efforts to build and protect goodwill. Note how the reminders of inequality in the following examples hamper communication:

Provide straightforward translations for the following doublespeak words and phrases:

- aerial ordinance
- detainee
- ethnic cleansing
- person of interest

- regime change
- rightsize
- take down
- vertically deployed anti-personnel devices

Check your answers and read other examples of doublespeak at the following website:

http://www.sourcewatch.org/wiki.phtml?title=Doublespeak

You may link to this URL or other updated sites from the text support site.

Ineffective Example

Since I took a leadership role in this project, the team's performance has improved.

As director of marketing, I will decide whether your product proposal has merit.

You were not selected, as we are looking for a candidate with exceptional skills.

A demeaning expression (sometimes called a *dysphemism*) makes an idea seem negative or disrespectful. Avoid demeaning expressions because they divert attention from the real message to emotional issues that have little to do with the message. Many examples can be taken as contempt for an occupation or a specific job/position (bean counters for accountants, ambulance chasers for lawyers, spin doctors for politicians or public relations directors, and shrinks for psychiatrists). Like words that attack races or nationalities, words that ridicule occupations work against a communicator's purpose. Many demeaning expressions are common across regions, ages, and perhaps even cultures. Some demeaning expressions belong to a

Effective communicators use clear, jargon-free language that can be easily understood by non-native readers and can be easily translated.

particular company; for example, "turtles" was coined in one firm to mock first-year employees for the slow pace at which they completed their work. One software sales representative assured a group of executives that the system he was selling was no "Mickey Mouse system." The cost of using a seemingly innocent statement resulted in the loss of a very large account—Walt Disney Studios. Focus on using respectful expressions that build and protect goodwill.

Use Connotative Tone Cautiously

Human relations can suffer when connotative words are inadvertently or intentionally used instead of denotative words. The **denotative meaning** of a word is the literal meaning that most people assign to it. The **connotative meaning** is the literal meaning plus an extra message that reveals the speaker's or writer's qualitative judgment, as shown in this example:

Connotative Meaning with Negative Meaning	Denotative Meaning (Preferred)
Another <u>gripe session</u> has been scheduled for tomorrow.	Another <u>employee forum</u> has been scheduled for tomorrow.

What connotative message is conveyed in "Have you read the latest commandment from above?" How might you rewrite the sentence using the denotative meaning?

The connotative meaning of "gripe session" carries an additional message that the writer has a bias against employee forums. The connotation may needlessly introduce thoughts about whether employee forums are beneficial and distract the receiver from paying sufficient attention to statements that follow. Connotations, like metacommunications discussed in Chapter 2, involve messages that are implied. In the preceding example, the connotation seems to be more harmful than helpful.

At times, however, connotations can be helpful, as seen in the following examples:

Connotative Meaning with Positive Meaning (Preferred)	Denotative Meaning
Our <u>corporate think tank</u> has developed an outstanding production process.	<u>Research and Development</u> has developed an outstanding production process.
Julia's likable personality <u>has made her a miracle worker</u> at contract negotiation.	Julia's likable personality is <u>beneficial</u> in contract negotiation.

In crafting business messages, rely mainly on denotative or connotative words that will be interpreted in a positive manner. To be sure that your connotative words are understood and will generate goodwill, consider your audience, the context, and the timing of the message.

- *Connotative words may be more easily misinterpreted than denotative words.* Because of differences in peoples' perceptions based on their life experiences, words that are perceived positively by one person may be perceived negatively by another. In some cases, the receiver may simply not understand the connotative words; they are "clueless" to the intended message. Damaged human relations occur when managers repeatedly convey connotative messages without considering whether employees can interpret the meanings as they are intended.

- *The appropriateness of connotations varies with the audience to which they are addressed and the context in which they appear.* For example, referring to a car as a "foreign job" or "sweet" might be received differently by teenagers than by senior citizens. Such expressions are less appropriate in a research report than in a popular magazine.

Use Specific Language Appropriately

Choose precise, vigorous words that the receiver will find exciting and will remember.

To help the receiver understand your message easily, select words that paint intense, colorful word pictures. Creating clear mental images adds energy and imagination to your message, thus increasing its overall impact.

General	*Specific (Preferred)*
Congratulations on your <u>recent honor</u>.	Congratulations on being named <u>employee of the month</u>.
Complete the report <u>as soon as possible</u>.	Complete the report <u>by May 2</u>.
Sales <u>skyrocketed</u> this quarter.	Sales <u>increased 10 percent</u> this quarter.

Sometimes, using general statements can be useful in building and protecting goodwill. General words keep negative ideas from getting more emphasis than they deserve. In addition, senders who don't have specific information or for some reason don't want to divulge it use general words.

General (Preferred)	*Specific*
Thank you for the explanation of your <u>financial status</u>.	Thank you for writing me about your <u>problems with your creditors and the possibility of filing bankruptcy</u>.
Greg told me about <u>what happened last week</u>.	Greg told me about the <u>tragedy in your family</u>.

Use Bias-Free Language

Being responsive to individual differences requires you to make a conscious effort to use bias-free (nondiscriminatory) language. Using language that does not exclude, stereotype, or offend others permits them to focus on your message rather than to question your sensitivity. Goodwill can be damaged when biased statements are made related to gender, race or ethnicity, religion, age, or disability.

Avoid Gender Bias. The following guidelines will help you avoid gender bias:

1. ***Avoid referring to men and women in stereotyped roles and occupations.*** The use of *he* to refer to anyone in a group was once standard and accepted; however, this usage is considered insensitive and, to some, offensive. Therefore, do not use the pronoun *he* when referring to a person in a group that may include women or the pronoun *she* to refer to a group that may include men; otherwise you may unintentionally communicate an insensitive message that only women or only men can perform certain tasks or serve in certain professions. Follow these four approaches to avoid gender bias:

Sensitive communicators use bias-free language.

Guideline	*Gender-Biased*	*Improved*
Avoid using a pronoun:	Each employee must submit <u>his</u> completed health report.	Each employees must submit a completed health report.

© Orlin Wagner/AP Photo

Openness a "Hallmark" at Hallmark Cards, Inc.

An extensive communications audit occurred at Hallmark Cards a few years ago. Despite the fact that Hallmark was one of the top brand names in the United States for decades, greeting card sales in the early and mid-90s lagged as time-conscious consumers turned to alternative means of keeping in touch. Increased use of email, cell phone calling, and e-card options provided viable alternatives to traditional greeting cards. In addition, a changing retail landscape saw specialty card shops giving way to mega-retailers and deep-discount shops. Due to Hallmark's private ownership and highly competitive retail/intellectual property environment, senior management had traditionally shared little with employees in terms of company finances, business plans, and market challenges. Management's guarded approach to communication had resulted in declining trust levels among employees. Director of Corporate Communications Dean Rodenbough knew that changes were needed in marketing strategy and in internal communications.

With economic conditions showing that significant changes were imminent, Rodenbough and other senior managers knew they had to both prepare and rally the work force. Initial focus group research with customers, vendors, suppliers, subsidiary leadership, and employees helped Hallmark identify behaviors that it wanted to integrate into its "new" corporate culture. A communication audit, which took approximately 12 months to complete, resulted in the formation of several action steps designed to assist the company in communicating openly, directly, and honestly. According to Vicci Rodgers of The Rodgers Group, and a member of the audit team, "Open, honest

> *Open, honest communication is becoming the norm, it's no longer the exception, at Hallmark."*

Spotlight Communicator: Dean Rodenbough

DIRECTOR OF CORPORATE COMMUNICATIONS, HALLMARK CORPORATION

communication is becoming the norm, it's no longer the exception, at Hallmark."[16]

One change implemented at Hallmark was to share with all employees the company's long-term vision, strategy, and financial goals. Another change was to focus more closely on internal communication tools. Publications produced primarily for external audiences had required extensive support from the editorial and design staff, limiting the resources available for key internal communication programs. As part of the transformed culture, Hallmark discontinued some of its external communication tools and repositioned its long-standing *Noon News* employee newsletter to devote space to candid commentary about the communication audit and its findings. An additional change affected information shared over the company's intranet. An intranet manager and an online editor were also hired to enhance the intranet's appeal, and employees now have access to information on monthly revenue and earnings results and other performance measures. Hallmark achieved its goals for operating profit during this period of cultural change. Although the company's improved earnings cannot be attributed completely to improved internal communication, Hallmark has a clear understanding of the vital role communication plays in successful company performance.[17]

Applying What You Have Learned

1. How has cultural change impacted the mission and activities of Hallmark?

2. Dean Rodenbough is quoted as saying that "the CEO is traditionally the voice of any major decision impacting our employees or one of our businesses and is our preferred spokesperson." If so, why does Hallmark need a Director of Corporate Communications? Discuss your response in class or online.

http://www.hallmark.com

REFER TO SHOWCASE, PART 3, ON PAGE 103, FOR ADVICE FROM HALLMARK ON SAYING JUST THE RIGHT THING.

Hallmark uses its intranet and employee newsletter, Noon News, to communicate valuable information to employees. Note the scope of valuable information communicated to employees through the Hallmark intranet and a sample issue of Noon News touting a shared marketing campaign with Starbucks.

Repeat the noun:	the courtesy of your guide. Ask <u>him</u> to . . .	the courtesy of your <u>guide</u>. Ask the <u>guide</u> to . . .
Use a plural noun:	A nurse must complete <u>her</u> in-service training to update <u>her</u> certification.	Nurses must complete in-service training to update <u>their</u> certification.
Use pronouns from both genders (when necessary, but not repeatedly):	Just call the manager. <u>He</u> will in turn . . .	Just call the manager. <u>He or she</u> will in turn . . .

2. Use occupational titles that reflect genuine sensitivity to gender. Note the gender-free titles that can be easily substituted to avoid bias:

Revise this statement to avoid gender bias: "Managers and their wives are invited to a retreat at Lake Tahoe."

Gender-Biased	*Gender-Free*
waiter or waitress	server
foreman	supervisor
working mother	working parent

Provide other examples of gender-biased terms and appropriate gender-free alternatives.

3. Avoid designating an occupation by gender. For example, omit "woman" in "A woman doctor has initiated this research." The doctor's profession, not the gender, is the point of the message. Similarly, avoid using the *-ess* ending to differentiate genders in an occupation:

Gender-Biased	*Gender-Free*
hostess	host
actress	actor

What actions are companies taking to raise employee awareness of diversity issues?

4. Avoid using expressions that may be perceived to be gender-biased. Avoid commonly used expressions in which "man" represents all humanity, such as "To go where no man has gone before," and stereotypical characteristics, such as "man hours," "man-made goods," and "work of four strong men." Note the improvements made in the following examples by eliminating the potentially offensive words.

Gender-Biased	Improved
Preparing the annual report is a <u>man-sized</u> task.	Preparing the annual report is an <u>enormous</u> task.
Luke is the best <u>man</u> for the job.	Trey is the best <u>person</u> for the job.

Avoid Racial or Ethnic Bias. Include racial or ethnic identification only when relevant and avoid referring to these groups in stereotypical ways.

Racially or Ethnically Biased	Improved
Submit the request to Alfonso Perez, the <u>Spanish</u> clerk in Payroll.	Submit the request to Alfonso Perez, the clerk in Payroll.
Dan's <u>Irish</u> temper flared today.	Dan's temper flared today.

Avoid Age Bias. Include age only when relevant and avoid demeaning expressions related to age.

Give examples of words and phrases that can be used to avoid race, ethnicity, or disability bias.

Age-Biased	Improved
Jeremy Cravens, the <u>55-year-old</u> president of Monroe Bank, has resigned.	Jeremy Cravens, the president of Monroe Bank, has resigned.

Avoid Disability Bias. When communicating about people with disabilities, use people-first language. That is, refer to the person first and the disability second so that focus is appropriately placed on the person's ability rather than on the disability. Also avoid words with negative or judgmental connotations, such as *handicap*, *unfortunate*, *afflicted*, and *victim*. When describing people without disabilities, use the word *typical* rather than *normal*; otherwise you may inadvertently imply that people with disabilities are abnormal. Consider these more sensitive revisions:

Insensitive	Sensitive (People-First)
<u>Blind</u> employees receive . . .	Employees <u>with vision impairments</u> receive . . .
The elevator is for the exclusive use of <u>handicapped</u> employees and should not be used by <u>normal</u> employees.	The elevator is for the exclusive use of employees <u>with disabilities</u>.

Use Contemporary Language

Business messages should reflect correct, standard English and contemporary language used in a professional business setting. Outdated expressions and dull clichés reduce the effectiveness of a message and the credibility of a communicator.

Eliminate Outdated Expressions

Using outdated expressions will give your message a dull, stuffy, unnatural tone. Instead, substitute fresh, original expressions that reflect today's language patterns.

Outdated Expressions	Improvement
<u>Pursuant to your request</u>, the physical inventory has been scheduled for May 3.	<u>As you requested</u>, the physical inventory has been scheduled for May 3.
<u>Enclosed please find</u> a copy of my transcript.	The <u>enclosed</u> transcript should answer your questions.
<u>Very truly yours</u> (used as the complimentary close in a letter)	Sincerely

Eliminate Clichés

At what point does a word become a cliché? Substitute an original word for "The ball is in your court."

Clichés, overused expressions, are common in our everyday conversations and in business messages. These handy verbal shortcuts are convenient, quick, easy to use, and often include simple metaphors and analogies that effectively communicate the most basic idea or emotion or the most complex business concept. However, writers and speakers who routinely use stale clichés may be perceived as unoriginal, unimaginative, lazy, and perhaps even disrespectful. Less frequently used words capture the receiver's attention because they are original, fresh, and interesting.

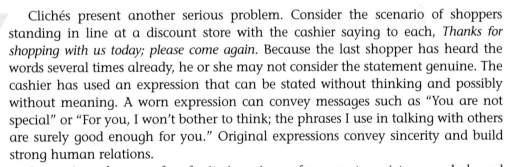

Cliché	Improvement
Pushed (or stretched) the envelope	Took a risk or considered a new option
Skin in the game	Commited to the project
Cover all the bases	Get agreement/input from everyone
That sucks!	That's unacceptable/needs improvement

In groups, generate a list of clichés used by friends, instructors, or coworkers. How do you feel when these expressions are used frequently?

Clichés present another serious problem. Consider the scenario of shoppers standing in line at a discount store with the cashier saying to each, *Thanks for shopping with us today; please come again.* Because the last shopper has heard the words several times already, he or she may not consider the statement genuine. The cashier has used an expression that can be stated without thinking and possibly without meaning. A worn expression can convey messages such as "You are not special" or "For you, I won't bother to think; the phrases I use in talking with others are surely good enough for you." Original expressions convey sincerity and build strong human relations.

Increasing tolerance of profanity is an issue of concern to society as a whole and also for employers and employees as they communicate at work. You must consider the potential business liabilities and legal implications resulting from the use of profanity that may offend others or create a hostile work environment. Recognize that minimizing or eliminating profanity is another important way you must adapt your language for communicating effectively and fostering human relations in a professional setting. The accompanying Strategic Forces feature, "E-Cards Offer Greeting Alternatives," explores yet another challenge for contemporary communication, the effective use of e-cards as alternatives for traditional greetings.

Use Simple, Informal Words

Business writers prefer simple, informal words that are readily understood and less distracting than more difficult, formal words. If a receiver questions the sender's

CHANGING TECHNOLOGY

E-Cards Offer Greeting Alternatives

They are fun and clever, and better yet, they arrive instantly. Electronic greeting cards are widely available on the Internet, many for free, and can be sent easily to individuals or groups.

Blue Mountain is the largest electronic greeting card site on the Web and has plenty of cards to choose from. Beginning as a free site, Blue Mountain now offers a limited free selection along with an extensive assortment of greetings on a subscription basis. You can add music and pick from greetings that range from sentimental to businesslike or customize your message. Another feature is the ability to send cards in several languages—a real plus in a world that is becoming ever smaller.

Many card sites allow the sender to "attach" gifts; the Hallmark website allows customers to send free e-cards and include a gift certificate to one of nearly 300 merchants. Distinctiveness has led to the growing popularity of Regards.com. As with some other sites, you can use your own photos and images to create an original design or select one of its uniquely animated cards, some of which are

so elaborate that they are like sending tiny cartoons. Attempting to become the number one web stop, Amazon.com also has electronic greeting cards, perhaps some of the best on the Web. Another site called Digital Greetings allows you to create a card in a simple, step-by-step process. You pick out illustrations, headlines, and colors, with the result being a card that you created yourself.[18] Perfect Greetings is able to offer free card service because it is sustained by its business sponsors. To send a card, customers must click on one of three randomly generated ads and read about a business offering while their card processing is completed.

Of course, if you're really international, you should check out the Digital Postcard. A wide array of languages is available, including Arabic and Turkish, and cards can be customized from a database of more than 1,000 photos. You can also include a link to a web page with your card, as well as upload a music or voice file.

In response to worries about the network bandwidth that

electronic greeting cards might consume, some sites sell compressed cards that load faster and take up fewer computer resources. Managers, however, are typically more concerned with lost worker productivity that may result as more workers gain access to the Internet. Companies that offer digital greeting cards, however, maintain that these products have a place in business. For example, they can be used to inform clients of an office move or thank clients in a less costly, faster manner than with the traditional alternative of addressing and mailing company cards.

Application

Visit the following greeting card sites:

http://www.bluemountain.com/
http://www.regards.com/
http://www.cards.amazon.com/
http://www.digitalgreetings.com/
http://www.perfectgreetings.com
http://www.hallmark.com

Rate the sites according to their suitability for sending business greetings. What considerations should be made when deciding whether to send an electronic greeting card rather than a traditional card or short typed message to a client or business associate?

motive for using formal words, the impact of the message may be diminished. Likewise, the impact would be diminished if the receiver questioned a sender's use of simple, informal words. That distraction is unlikely, however, if the message contains good ideas that are well organized and well supported. Under these conditions, simple words enable a receiver to understand the message clearly and quickly.

To illustrate, consider the unnecessary complexity of a notice that appeared on a corporate bulletin board: "Employees impacted by the strike are encouraged to utilize the hot line number to arrange for alternative transportation to work. Should you encounter difficulties in arranging for alternative transportation to work, please contact your immediate supervisor." A simple, easy-to-read revision would be, "If you can't get to work, call the hot line or your supervisor."[20] For further illustration, note the added clarity of the following words:

Formal Words	Informal Words
terminate	end
procure	get
remunerate	pay
corroborate	support

DIVERSITY CHALLENGES

Using words that have more than two or three syllables when they are the most appropriate is acceptable. However, you should avoid regular use of a long, infrequently used word when a simpler, more common word has the same meaning. Professionals in some fields often use specialized terminology, referred to as *jargon,* when communicating with colleagues in the same field. In this case, the audience is likely to understand the words, and using the jargon saves time. However, when communicating with people outside the field, professionals should select simple, common words to convey messages. Using clear, jargon-free language that can be readily understood by non-native recipients and easily translated is especially important in international communication.

You should build your vocabulary so that you can use just the right word for expressing an idea and can understand what others have said. Just remember the purpose of business messages is not to advertise a knowledge of infrequently used words but to transmit a clear and tactful message. For the informal communication practiced in business, use simple words instead of more complicated words that have the same meaning.

Communicate Concisely

Concise communication includes all relevant details in the fewest possible words. Abraham Lincoln's two-minute Gettysburg Address is a premier example of concise communication. Mark Twain alluded to the skill needed to write concisely when he said, "I would have written a shorter book if I had had time."

Some executives have reported that they read memos that are two paragraphs long but may only skim or discard longer ones. Yet it's clear that this survival technique can lead to a vital message being discarded or misread. Concise writing is essential for information workers struggling to handle the avalanche of information created by technological advances and other factors. Concise messages save time and money for both the sender and the receiver. The receiver's attention is directed toward the important details and is not distracted by excessive words and details.

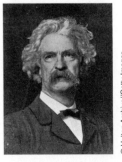

Having an extensive vocabulary at your disposal will aid you in choosing precise words for particular situations. Visit the College Board Vocabulary quizzing site at http://iteslj.org/v/e/jb-college.html. You may link to this URL or other updated sites from the text support site.

Quiz yourself on the first 25 terms that are generated. Write down the words for which you chose an incorrect definition. Provide email feedback to your instructor as to your percentage of correct responses and the words that gave you trouble. If directed by your instructor, continue to quiz on this site for the remainder of the course term.

The following techniques will produce concise messages:

In groups, generate a list of wordy phrases you have heard. Describe ways to simplify ideas in writing and speaking.

- ***Eliminate redundancies.*** A **redundancy** is a phrase in which one word unnecessarily repeats an idea contained in an accompanying word. "Exactly identical" and "past history" are redundant because both words have the same meaning; only "identical" and "history" are needed. To correct "3 p.m. in the afternoon," say "3 p.m." or "three o'clock in the afternoon." A few of the many redundancies in business writing are shown in the following list. Be conscious of redundancies in your speech and writing patterns.

Redundancies to Avoid	
Needless repetition:	advance forward, it goes without saying, best ever, cash money, important essentials, each and every, dollar amount, pick and choose
Unneeded modifiers:	actual experience, brief summary, complete stop, collaborate together, disappear from sight, honest truth, trickle down, month of May, pair of twins, personal opinion, red in color, severe crisis
Repeated acronyms:	ATM Machine, PIN Number, SAT tests, SIC code

How can the effective communicator restate without being redundant?

Redundancy is not to be confused with repetition. In a sentence or paragraph, you may need to use a certain word again. When repetition serves a specific purpose, it is not an error. Redundancy serves no purpose and *is* an error.

- ***Use active voice to reduce the number of words.*** Passive voice typically adds unnecessary words, such as prepositional phrases. Compare the sentence length in each of these examples:

Passive Voice	*Active Voice*
The documentation was prepared by the systems analyst.	The systems analyst prepared the documentation.
The loan approval procedures were revised by the loan officer.	The loan officer revised the loan approval procedures.

- ***Review the main purpose of your writing and identify relevant details needed for the receiver to understand and take necessary action.*** More information is not necessarily better information. You may be so involved and perhaps so enthusiastic about your message that you believe the receiver needs to know everything that you know. Or perhaps you just need to devote more time to audience analysis and empathy.

Nonconcise letters sometimes begin with an "empty acknowledgment." Give some examples of such openings.

- ***Eliminate clichés that are often wordy and not necessary to understand the message.*** For example, "Thank you for your letter," "I am writing to," "May I take this opportunity," "It has come to my attention," and "We wish to inform you" only delay the major purpose of the message.

- ***Do not restate ideas that are sufficiently implied.*** Notice how the following sentences are improved when ideas are implied. The revised sentences are concise, yet the meaning is not affected.

Wordy	Concise
She <u>took</u> the Internet marketing course and <u>passed</u> it.	She passed the Internet marketing course.
The editor <u>checked</u> the advertisement and <u>found</u> three glaring errors.	The editor found three glaring errors in the advertisement.

Attention to careful revision of the first draft will eliminate most wordiness.

- ***Shorten sentences by using suffixes or prefixes, making changes in word form, or substituting precise words for phrases.*** In the following examples, the expressions in the right column provide useful techniques for saving space and being concise. However, the examples in the left column are not grammatically incorrect or forbidden from use. In fact, sometimes their use provides just the right *emphasis*.

Wordy	Concise
She was a manager <u>who was courteous to others</u>.	She was a <u>courteous</u> manager.
He waited <u>in an impatient manner</u>.	He waited <u>impatiently</u>.
The production manager disregards methods considered <u>to be of no use</u>.	The production manager disregards <u>useless</u> methods.
Sales staff <u>with high energy levels</u> . . .	<u>Energetic</u> sales staff . . .
. . . arranged <u>according to the alphabet</u>	. . . arranged <u>alphabetically</u> . . .

- ***Use a compound adjective.*** By using the compound adjective, you can reduce the number of words required to express your ideas and thus save the reader a little time.

Wordy	Concise
The document requires language that is <u>gender-neutral</u>. . .	The document requires <u>gender-neutral</u> language.
B. J. Dahl, <u>who holds the highest rank</u> at Medder Enterprises, is . . .	B. J. Dahl, the <u>highest-ranking official</u> at Medder Enterprises, is . . .
His policy <u>of going slowly</u> was well received.	His <u>go-slow</u> policy was well received.

Project a Positive, Tactful Tone

Being adept at communicating negative information will give you the confidence you need to handle sensitive situations in a positive, constructive manner. The following suggestions reduce the sting of an unpleasant thought:

- ***State ideas using positive language.*** Rely mainly on positive words—words that speak of what can be done instead of what cannot be done, of the pleasant instead of the unpleasant. In each of the following pairs, both sentences are sufficiently clear, but the positive words in the improved sentences make the message more diplomatic and promote positive human relations.

Negative Tone	Positive Tone
<u>Don't forget</u> to submit your time and expense report.	Remember to submit your time and expense report.
We <u>cannot</u> ship your order until you send us full specifications.	You will receive your order as soon as you send us full specifications.
You <u>neglected</u> to indicate the specifications for Part No. 332-3.	Please send specifications for Part No. 332-3 so your order can be finalized.

Positive words are normally preferred, but sometimes negative words are more effective in achieving the dual goals of *clarity* and positive *human relations*. For example, addition of negative words can sharpen a contrast (and thus increase clarity):

> Use an oil-based paint for this purpose; do not use latex.
>
> Final copies are to be printed using a laser printer; ink-jet print is not acceptable.

Think of examples of negative language you have heard (or used) that could easily be stated using positive words.

When pleasant, positive words have not brought desired results, negative words may be justified. For example, a supervisor may have used positive words to instruct an accounts payable clerk to verify that the unit price on the invoice matches the unit price on the purchase order. Discovering later that the clerk is not verifying the invoices correctly, the supervisor may use negative words such as "*No,* that's the *wrong way*" to demonstrate once more, and explain. If the clerk continues to complete the task incorrectly, the supervisor may feel justified in using even stronger negative words. The clerk may need the emotional jolt that negative words can provide.

What advice would you give a businessperson for balancing tact and assertiveness?

- **Avoid using second person when stating negative ideas.** Avoid second person for presenting unpleasant ideas, but use second person for presenting pleasant ideas. Note the following examples:

Pleasant idea (second person preferred)	You substantiated your argument sufficiently.	*The person will appreciate the emphasis placed on his or her excellent performance.*
Unpleasant idea (third person preferred)	This report contains numerous mistakes.	*"You made numerous mistakes on this page" directs undiplomatic attention to the person who made the mistakes.*

However, use of second person with negative ideas is an acceptable technique on the rare occasions when the purpose is to jolt the receiver by emphasizing a negative.

- **Use passive voice to convey negative ideas.** Presenting an unpleasant thought emphatically (as active verbs do) makes human relations difficult. Compare the tone of the following negative thoughts written in active and passive voices:

Active Voice	Passive Voice Preferred for Negative Ideas
Melissa did not proofread the bid proposal carefully.	The bid proposal lacked careful proofreading.
Melissa completed the bid two weeks behind schedule.	The bid was completed two weeks behind schedule.

Because the subject of each active sentence is the doer, the sentences are emphatic. Since the idea is negative, Melissa probably would appreciate being taken out of the picture. The passive voice sentences place more emphasis on the job than on who failed to complete it; they retain the essential ideas, but the ideas seem less irritating. For negative ideas, use passive voice. Just as emphasis on negatives hinders human relations, emphasis on positives promotes human relations. Which sentence makes the positive idea more vivid?

Passive Voice	Active Voice Preferred for Positive Ideas
The bid was completed ahead of time.	Melissa completed the bid ahead of schedule.

Compose another sentence that uses subjunctive mood to de-emphasize a negative idea.

Because "Melissa" is the subject of the active-voice sentence, the receiver can easily envision the action. Pleasant thoughts deserve emphasis. For presenting positive ideas, use active voice. Active and passive voice are discussed in greater detail in the "Write Powerful Sentences" section in Chapter 4.

- *Use the subjunctive mood.* Sometimes the tone of a message can be improved by switching to the subjunctive mood. **Subjunctive sentences** speak of a wish, necessity, doubt, or condition contrary to fact and employ such conditional expressions as *I wish, as if, could, would, might,* and *wish.* In the following examples, the sentence in the right column conveys a negative idea in positive language, which is more diplomatic than negative language.

Negative Tone	Subjunctive Mood Conveys Positive Tone
I <u>cannot</u> approve your transfer to our overseas operation.	If positions <u>were</u> available in our overseas operation, I <u>would</u> approve your transfer.
I am <u>unable</u> to accept your invitation to speak.	I <u>could</u> accept your invitation to speak only if our scheduled speaker <u>were</u> to cancel.
I <u>cannot</u> accept the consultant's recommendation.	I <u>wish</u> I <u>could</u> accept the consultant's recommendation.

Sentences in subjunctive mood often include a reason that makes the negative idea seems less objectionable, and thus improves the tone. Tone is important, but clarity is even more important. The revised sentence in each of the preceding pairs sufficiently *implies* the unpleasant idea without stating it directly. If for any reason a writer suspects the implication is not sufficiently strong, a direct statement in negative terms is preferable.

- *Include a pleasant statement in the same sentence.* A pleasant idea is included in the following examples to improve the tone:

Negative Tone	Positive Tone
Your personnel ratings for communication ability and team skills were satisfactory.	Your personnel ratings for communication ability and team skills were satisfactory, but <u>your rate for technical competence was excellent</u>.
Because of increased taxes and insurance, you are obligated to increase your monthly payments.	Because of increased taxes and insurance, your monthly payments will increase by $50; however, <u>your home has increased in value at the monthly rate of $150</u>.

Step 4: Organizing the Message

Objective 4

Recognize the importance of organizing a message before writing the first draft.

After you have identified the specific ways you must adapt the message to your specific audience, you are ready to organize your message. In a discussion of communication, the word *organize* means "the act of dividing a topic into parts and arranging them in an appropriate sequence." Before undertaking this process, you must be convinced that the message is the right message—that it is complete, accurate, fair, reasonable, ethical, and logical. If it doesn't meet these standards, it should not be sent. Good organization and good writing or speaking cannot be expected to compensate for a bad decision.

If you organize and write simultaneously, the task seems hopelessly complicated. Writing is much easier if questions about the organization of the message are answered first: What is the purpose of the message, what is the receiver's likely reaction, and should the message begin with the main point? Once these decisions have been made, you can concentrate on expressing ideas effectively.

Outline to Benefit the Sender and the Receiver

When a topic is divided into parts, some parts will be recognized as central ideas and the others as minor ideas (details). The process of identifying these ideas and arranging them in the right sequence is known as **outlining.** Outlining *before* communicating provides numerous benefits:

- *Encourages accuracy and brevity.* Outlining reduces the chance of leaving out an essential idea or including an unessential idea.

- *Permits concentration on one phase at a time.* Having focused separately on (a) the ideas that need to be included, (b) the distinction between major and minor ideas, and (c) the sequence of ideas, total concentration can now be focused on the next challenge—expressing.

- *Saves time in structuring ideas.* With questions about which ideas to include and their proper sequence already answered, little time is lost in moving from one point to the next.

How can the business communicator make sure the message outline is a time saver and not a time waster?

- *Provides a psychological lift.* The feeling of success gained in preparing the outline increases confidence that the next step—writing or speaking—will be successful, too.

- *Facilitates emphasis and de-emphasis.* Although each sentence makes its contribution to the message, some sentences need to stand out more vividly in the receiver's mind than others. An effective outline ensures that important points will appear in emphatic positions.

The preceding benefits derived from outlining are sender oriented. Because a message has been well outlined, receivers benefit, too:

- The message is more concise and accurate.

- Relationships between ideas are easier to distinguish and remember.

- Reaction to the message and its sender is more likely to be positive.

A receiver's reaction to a message is strongly influenced by the sequence in which ideas are presented. A beginning sentence or an ending sentence is in an emphatic position. (Other emphasis techniques are explained later in this chapter.) Throughout this text, you will see that outlining (organizing) is important.

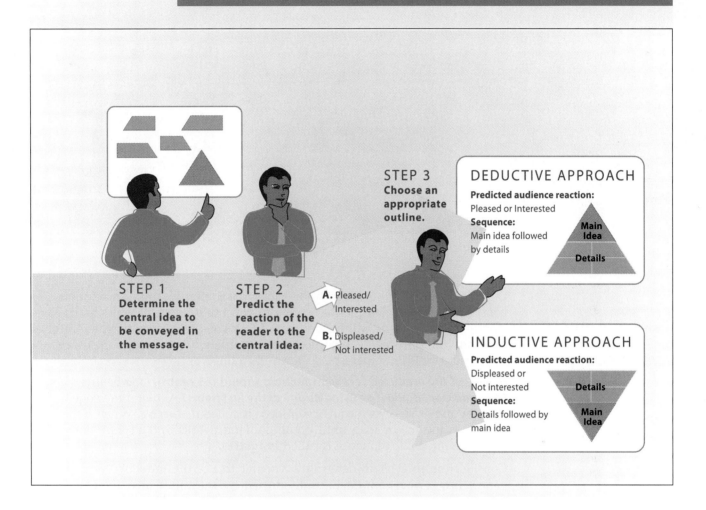

Sequence Ideas to Achieve Desired Goals

Objective 5

Select the appropriate message outline (deductive or inductive) for developing messages to achieve the desired response.

When planning your communication, you should strive for an outline that will serve you in much the same way a blueprint serves a builder or an itinerary serves a traveler. Organizing your message first will ensure that your ideas are presented clearly and logically and all vital components are included. To facilitate your determining an appropriate sequence for a business document or presentation, follow the three-step process illustrated in Figure 3-3. This process involves answering the following questions in this order:

Use the deductive sequence for positive and routine messages; use the inductive sequence for negative and persuasive messages.

1. *What is the central idea of the message?* Think about the *reason* you are writing or speaking—the first step in the communication process. What is your purpose—to extend a job offer, decline an invitation, or seek support for an innovative project? The purpose is the central idea of your message. You might think of it as a message condensed into a one-sentence telegram.

2. *What is the most likely receiver reaction to the message?* Ask, "If I were the one receiving the message I am preparing to send, what would *my* reaction be?" Because you would react with pleasure to good news and displeasure to bad news, you can reasonably assume a receiver's reaction would be similar. Recall

Assume you are to give a presentation on wireless digital cameras, cameras with the ability to off-load pictures to a PC or website via Wi-Fi. Read the following article available through the Business & Company Resource Center at http://bcrc.swlearning.com or from another database available from your campus library:

Sullivan, T. (2005, December 27). Digital cameras go wireless. PC Magazine, 24(23), 46-47.

After reading the article, decide which one you think is the superior product and develop your presentation to persuasively convince your audience of the better choice. Develop two versions of your presentation outline, one in inductive and one in deductive order. You may want to refer to Chapter 12 for more information on preparing outlines.

In groups, discuss the appropriate sequence for a message (a) accepting an invitation to speak, (b) denying credit to a customer, and (c) commending an employee for exemplary performance.

the dual goals of a communicator: clarity and effective human relations. By considering anticipated receiver reaction, you build goodwill with the receiver. Almost every message will fit into one of four categories of anticipated receiver reaction: (1) pleasure, (2) displeasure, (3) interest but neither pleasure nor displeasure, or (4) no interest, as shown in Figure 3-3.

3. **In view of the predicted receiver reaction, should the central idea be listed first in the outline or should it be listed as one of the last items?** When a message begins with the major idea, the sequence of ideas is called **deductive.** When a message withholds the major idea until accompanying details and explanations have been presented, the sequence is called **inductive.**

Consider the receiver to determine whether to use the inductive or deductive sequence. If a receiver might be antagonized by the main idea in a deductive message, lead up to the main idea by making the message inductive. If a sender wants to encourage receiver involvement (to generate a little concern about where the details are leading), the inductive approach is recommended. Inductive organization can be especially effective if the main idea confirms the conclusion the receiver has drawn from the preceding details—a cause is worthy of support, an applicant should be interviewed for a job, a product/service should be selected, and so on. As you learn in later chapters about writing letters, memos, and email messages and about planning spoken communications, you will comprehend the benefits of using the appropriate outline for each receiver reaction:

Deductive Order (main idea first)	Inductive Order (details first)
When the message will *please* the receiver	When the message will *displease* the receiver
When the message is *routine* (will not please nor displease)	When the receiver *may not be interested* (will need to be persuaded)

For determining the sequence of minor ideas that accompany the major idea, the following bases for idea sequence are common:

- **Time.** When writing a memo or email about a series of events or a process, paragraphs proceed from the first step through the last step.

Hallmark Tips for Writing Business Greetings

Hallmark has been helping people say the right thing at the right time for nearly 100 years. Getting and sending greeting cards make people feel good. But the "warm fuzzy" responses that make greeting cards so effective can also make some professional types a little nervous, especially if you are used to keeping in touch through phone calls, email, memos, and other less personal types of communication. If you are uneasy about using cards to stay in touch, relax—Hallmark has some helpful suggestions to help you personalize your messages and say just the right thing.

- Visit the Hallmark website at http://www. hallmark.com and read "What to Say . . . and How to Say It." What advantages are offered by sending greeting card messages?

- Locate "Tips on Sending Business Greetings" on the Hallmark site. What tips did you find most helpful?

© Susan Van Etten

Activities

Referring to the chapter, read the Strategic Forces feature on e-cards. In a class discussion, compare the roles of traditional greeting cards and e-cards in conveying business messages. Does audience impact differ? If so, how?

http://www.hallmark.com

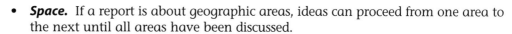

- ***Space.*** If a report is about geographic areas, ideas can proceed from one area to the next until all areas have been discussed.

- ***Familiarity.*** If a topic is complicated, the presentation can begin with a known or easy-to-understand point and proceed to progressively more difficult points.

- ***Importance.*** In analytical reports in which major decision-making factors are presented, the factors can be presented in order of most important to least important, or vice versa.

- ***Value.*** If a presentation involves major factors with monetary values, paragraphs can proceed from those with greatest values to those with least values, or vice versa.

The same organizational patterns are recommended for written and spoken communication. These patterns are applicable in email messages, letters, memos, and reports.

Summary

1. **Identify the purpose of the message and the appropriate channel.**

   Writing is a systematic process that begins by determining the purpose of the message (central idea) and identifying how the central idea will affect the receiver. In view of its effect on the receiver, you can determine the appropriate channel for sending a particular message (e.g., face-to-face, telephone, letter/memo, email, voice mail, or fax).

2. **Develop clear perceptions of the audience to enhance the impact of the communication and human relations.**

   Before you compose the first draft, commit to overcoming perceptual barriers that will limit your ability to see an issue from multiple perspectives and thus plan an effective message. Then, consider all you know about the receiver, including age, economic level, educational/occupational background, culture, existing relationship, expectations, and needs.

3. **Apply techniques for adapting messages to the audience, including strategies for communicating ethically and responsibly.**

   The insights you gain from seeking to understand your receiver will allow you to adapt the message to fit the receiver's needs. Developing concise, sensitive messages that focus on the receiver's point of view will build and protect goodwill and demand the attention of the receiver. Communicating

   ethically and responsibly involves stating information truthfully and tactfully, eliminating embellishments or exaggerations, supporting viewpoints with objective facts from credible sources, and designing honest graphics.

4. **Recognize the importance of organizing a message before writing the first draft.**

   Outlining involves identifying the appropriate sequence of pertinent ideas. Outlining encourages brevity and accuracy, permits concentration on one phase at a time, saves writing time, increases confidence to complete the task, and facilitates appropriate emphasis of ideas. From a receiver's point of view, well-organized messages are easier to understand and promote a more positive attitude toward the sender.

5. **Select the appropriate message outline (deductive or inductive) for developing messages to achieve the desired response.**

   A part of the outlining process is deciding whether the message should be deductive (main idea first) or inductive (explanations and details first). The main idea is presented first and details follow when the receiver is expected to be pleased by the message and the message is routine and not likely to arouse a feeling of pleasure or displeasure. When the receiver can be expected to be displeased or not initially interested, explanations and details precede the main idea.

Chapter Review

1. Why is selecting an appropriate communication channel important to the overall effectiveness of the message? Provide two examples. (Obj. 1)

2. How does perception and audience analysis affect the communication process? What factors about the audience should you consider? (Obj. 2)

3. What differences in the ideals of the older and younger generations may explain communication clashes between these groups in the workplace? (Objs. 2, 3)

4. What value is gained from cultivating a "you attitude" in spoken and written messages? Give an example of a writer- and a reader-centered message to make your point. (Obj. 3)

5. Discuss five writing techniques that enable communicators to build and protect goodwill. (Obj. 3)

6. When is the use of a euphemism appropriate? Detrimental? Under what conditions are connotative words acceptable? Why are specific words generally preferred in business writing and speaking? In what situations would general words be preferred? (Obj. 3)

7. Provide five guidelines for projecting a positive, tactful tone. (Obj. 3)

8. Why is conciseness valued in business communication? Provide at least three suggestions for reducing word count without sacrificing content. (Obj. 3)

9. What primary benefits does the writer gain from outlining before writing or speaking? How does the receiver benefit? (Obj. 4)

10. What three questions assist a communicator in the decision to organize a message deductively or inductively? (Obj. 5)

Digging Deeper

1. What is empathy and how does it affect business communication? How are empathy and sympathy different?

2. Explain what is meant by writing to *express* and not to *impress*.

3. Discuss the merits of adopting the communication style of your supervisor or senior members of your work team.

Assessment

To check your understanding of the chapter, take the available online quizzes as directed by your instructor.

Check Your Communication | *Guidelines for Planning a Spoken or Written Message*

Focus on the Receiver's Point of View

- Present ideas from the receiver's point of view, conveying the tone the message is specifically for the receiver.
- Give sincere compliments.

Communicate Ethically and Responsibly

- Present information truthfully, honestly, and fairly.
- Include all information relevant to the receiver.
- Avoid exaggerating or embellishing facts.
- Use objective facts to support ideas.
- Design graphics that avoid distorting facts and relationships.
- Express ideas clearly and understandably.
- State ideas tactfully and positively to preserve the receiver's self-worth and to build future relationships.

Build and Protect Goodwill

- Use euphemisms to present unpleasant thoughts politely and positively. Avoid using euphemisms when they will be taken as excessive or sarcastic.
- Avoid doublespeak or corporate speak that confuses or misleads the receiver.
- Avoid using condescending or demeaning expressions.
- Rely mainly on denotative words. Use connotative words that will elicit a favorable reaction, are easily understood, and are appropriate for the setting.
- Choose vivid words that add clarity and interest to your message.
- Use bias-free language.
- Do not use the pronoun *he* when referring to a group of people that may include women or *she* when a group may include men.
- Avoid referring to men and women in stereotyped roles and occupations, using gender-biased occupational titles, or differentiating genders in an occupation.

- Avoid referring to groups (based on gender, race and ethnicity, age, religion, and disability) in stereotypical and insensitive ways.
- Do not emphasize race and ethnicity, age, religion, or disability when these factors are not relevant.

Convey a Positive, Tactful Tone

- Rely mainly on positive words that speak of what can be done instead of what cannot be done, of the pleasant instead of the unpleasant. Use negative words when the purpose is to sharpen contrast or when positive words have not evoked the desired reaction.
- Use second person and active voice to emphasize pleasant ideas. Avoid using second person for presenting negative ideas; instead, use third person and passive voice to de-emphasize the unpleasant.
- Consider stating an unpleasant thought in the subjunctive mood.

Use Simple, Contemporary Language

- Avoid clichés and outdated expressions that make your language seem unnatural and unoriginal.
- Use simple words for informal business messages instead of using more complicated words that have the same meaning.

Write Concisely

- Do not use redundancies—unnecessary repetition of an idea.
- Use active voice to shorten sentences.
- Avoid unnecessary details; omit ideas that can be implied.
- Shorten wordy sentences by using suffixes or prefixes, making changes in word form, or substituting precise words for phrases.

Activities

1. **Empathetic Attitude (Obj. 2)**

   Identify possible communication problems created because of a manager's lack of empathy when communicating to employees. Select a spokesperson to share your group's ideas.

   a. A manager for a U.S. firm, who has been transferred to the company's office in Japan, provides the following message to launch the marketing/production team's work on a new product:

"We really need to put our noses to the grindstone to launch this new product. I've been burning the midnight oil with my people in R&D, and I have some new ideas that need to be implemented before the competition catches on and the cat's out of the bag. So let's all hit the ground running. Keep me posted, and remember, my door is always open. Everybody got it?"

b. After months of uncertainty at Ramsey, Inc., a corporate official visits an office of the national corporation with the following response to concerned questions by mostly lower-wage technical and support staff regarding layoffs and office closures:

"We are realigning our resources company-wide to be more competitive in the marketplace. Our stock has been declining at an unpromising rate, but we are taking steps to ensure future market viability. Restructuring has begun at several levels. Corporate is aware of your concerns and will continue having these meetings to provide a forum for dialog."

c. After several trips to Mexico and nearly a year of negotiation to set up a joint venture, a U.S. partner faxed the final contract to the Mexican chief executive officer. The final contract included a request that the CEO personally guarantee the loan, a stipulation that had not been discussed previously.

2. **Appropriate Outline and Channel (Objs. 1, 2, 5)**

Complete the following analysis to determine whether a deductive or an inductive outline is appropriate for the following situations. Identify the channel you believe would be most appropriate for conveying this message; be prepared to justify your answer. Use the format shown in the following example.

Go to www.thomsonedu.com/bcomm/lehman for a downloadable version of this activity.

a. Seller to customer: An e-commerce site is promoting a special digital music subcription to its customers who recently purchased a portable music device.

b. To company from customer: An incorrect part ordered from a website must be exchanged. No return instructions were provided with the invoice.

c. Quality manager to production manager: Discontinue production until a flaw just discovered in the production process has been corrected.

d. Seller to customer: We cannot provide a free cellular phone upgrade until the service contract is renewed.

e. CEO to managers: Pension plans will be discontinued to new hires.

f. U.S. CEO to Canadian business partner: Delivery of promised shipment will be delayed due to inability to obtain raw products from a war-torn country.

g. Management to employees: A meeting to learn about the company's new stock option plan is announced.

h. Seller to customer: Refunds are being distributed to customers who purchased the Model DX laptop, which had a faulty board.

i. Seller to customer: Because of an increase in fuel cost, the company's price structure will increase beginning June 1.

j. Assistant to manager: The assistant has been asked by his manager to research an issue and respond immediately while the manager is still on the telephone with the customer.

k. Management to employees: A new policy prohibiting employees from smoking at work and at home is introduced as a means of managing rising health care costs.

l. Technology department to customer: The solution to a common problem users are encountering while upgrading software versions is made available to all current and prospective customers.

3. **Audience Analysis (Obj. 2)**

Write a brief analysis of the audience for each of the situations presented in Activity 2.

4. **Receiver-Centered Messages (Obj. 3)**

Revise the following sentences to emphasize the reader's viewpoint and the "you" attitude.

Go to www.thomsonedu.com/bcomm/lehman for a downloadable version of this activity.

a. We're requesting that members call us on weekdays from 9 a.m. to 5 p.m. Central Standard Time to confirm reservations.

b. Human Resources requires all employees who work with dangerous goods or hazardous materials to have a complete physical every year.

5. **Statements that Build and Protect Goodwill (Obj. 3)**

Revise the following sentences to eliminate a tone that will damage human relations. Identify the specific weakness in each sentence.

Go to www.thomsonedu.com/bcomm/lehman for a downloadable version of this activity.

a. Management expresses appreciation for all the maintenance engineers.

b. Although we strenuously continue to easily outclass our competitors on an enterprisewise level of actionability, our global customer care agents are experiencing a skill gap in terms of their abilities and knowledge in the area of satisfying customers, particularly when their first call response rate is measured against industry benchmarks

Situation	Recommended channel	Central idea	Likely receiver reaction
The annual merit raise has increased to 5 percent.	Mailed memo or email message; pleasant information that should reach all employees in a timely manner.	Inform employees of an increase in annual merit raise.	Deductive.

and their call resolution rate is compared to rates achieved by other entities in this space.[21]

c. As expected, the spin doctors fired a quick response to the complaints of the consumer advocacy group.

d. As anyone must surely know, an employee cannot be allowed to reconcile his/her own accounts.

e. The production manager harped on the new quality assurance regulations for nearly an hour.

f. An effective presenter is never surprised by the reaction of his audience.

g. Several patient satisfaction surveys have included negative comments about Jim McLaurin, a male ER nurse.

h. Our quadriplegic first-shift supervisor moves around the plant in a motorized wheelchair.

i. Obviously we had reached a Mexican standoff with the negotiations.

j. Josh Williams was recognized for his efforts.

6. Positive, Tactful Tone (Obj. 3)

Revise the following sentences to reduce the negative tone.

Go to www.thomsonedu.com/bcomm/lehman for a downloadable version of this activity.

a. The policyholder failed to alter his flexible spending deduction during the annual enrollment period.

b. You cannot receive benefits until after you have been with our company for three months.

c. You neglected to inform these potential buyers of the 10-day cancellation period.

7. Conversational Language (Obj. 3)

Substitute fresh, original expressions for each cliché or out-dated expression.

Go to www.thomsonedu.com/bcomm/lehman for a downloadable version of this activity.

a. Give me a minute here; I'm drinking from a fire hose.

b. Despite her talent and obvious potential, Kelly has pursued only McJobs since her arrival here from Florida.

c. We are in receipt of your letter of July 15.

8. Simple Words (Obj. 3)

Revise the following sentences using shorter, simpler words.

Go to www.thomsonedu.com/bcomm/lehman for a downloadable version of this activity.

a. Jan's dubious disappearance yesterday instigated a police investigation.

b. The attendees of the convocation concurred that it should terminate at the appointed hour.

c. We utilized an innovative device to restore the computer's video display terminal.

9. Conciseness (Obj. 3)

Revise the following sentences to eliminate redundancies and other wordy construction.

Go to www.thomsonedu.com/bcomm/lehman for a downloadable version of this activity.

a. Although some damage to the building was visible to the eye, we were directed by our attorneys not to repair or change anything until the adjuster made a damage assessment.

b. Ellen's past work history includes working as a sales clerk, waiting tables in a restaurant, and stocking shelves in a bookstore.

c. Dan was instructed to note any strange and unusual transactions completed in the recent past.

10. Adapting the Message to the Audience (Objs. 1–3)

Revise the following sentences by adapting the message to meet the audience's needs. Identify the specific weaknesses in each sentence.

Go to www.thomsonedu.com/bcomm/lehman for a downloadable version of this activity.

a. We want all employees to be familiar with OSHA requirements that pertain to their jobs.

b. Each project manager must complete the appropriate performance evaluation forms before being awarded his raise.

c. After the recent downsizing, most employees are beginning to feel like rats on a sinking ship.

d. Please be advised that the city's new smoke-free policy is effective on January 1.

e. Since I took a leadership role on this project, the team's performance has improved.

f. The grapevine has it that the company shrink is putting together more tests for us to take by the end of the year.

g. You failed to read the disclaimer on our website that clearly indicates that the transmitter you ordered does not work with older generation MP3 players. Unfortunately, we cannot honor your request for a refund.

h. Through strategic alliances and by internal expansion of programs, Lox Enterprises is seeking to develop a substantial market presence as the leading provider of management consulting services in Illinois and its neighboring states.

i. The best computers available for lease through corporate channels are horribly outdated.

j. The supervisor asked Quan to go back and make revisions to the final draft of the report so the data will be completely accurate.

Applications

Read	Think	Write	Speak	Collaborate

1. Diversity Awareness Strategies in Real Companies (Objs. 2, 3)

Conduct an online search to identify strategies companies have adopted to raise their employees' awareness of diversity in the workplace. In chart form, summarize the indexes you used to locate your articles, the companies you read about, and the successful strategies they have used to promote diversity.

2. Application of Empathy in Company Strategies (Objs. 2, 3)

Visit the website of a company in which you are interested to explore evidence of the company's empathy for its employees and customers/clients. Alternately, you may choose a company from Fortune's Best 100 Companies to Work For or Fortune's Most Admired Companies. In a short oral report, explain the role of empathy in the strategies you identified.

3. Ethical Communication Practices (Obj. 3)

Locate the following article from the Business & Company Resource Center (http://bcrc.swlearning.com) or another database from your campus library:

Williams, D. (2002, April). Un-spun: Ethical communication practices serve the public interest, *Communication World*, p. 27.

After reading the article, respond to the following questions:

a. What factors have contributed to the current decline in ethical and moral practices?

b. What is meant by the statement, "Businesses communicators aren't in the hero business"?

c. Describe briefly the code of ethics of the International Association for Business Communication.

d. How does this professional code relate to the general guidelines presented in the text for communicating ethically and responsibly?

Read	Think	Write	Speak	Collaborate

4. Choosing Communication Channels Wisely (Obj. 1)

Locate the following article from the Business & Company Resource Center (http://bcrc.swlearning.com) or another database from your campus library:

Gilbert, J. (2002, November). Click, call, or write? With so many ways to communicate, it's tough to know what's most appropriate for each sales situation. Here's how to choose. *Sales & Marketing Management*, 25.

After reading the article, compile a list of the advantages and recommended use for each communication channel. Refer to Figure 3–2 on page 76 for assistance in identifying channels and information for your analysis.

Go to www.thomsonedu.com/bcomm/lehman for a downloadable version of this activity.

5. Building Strong Interpersonal Skills (Objs. 1–3)

The guidelines presented in this chapter for adapting your message to convey sensitivity for the receiver are an excellent means for building the relationships and strong interpersonal skills needed in today's highly competitive global market and in diverse work teams. Identify a specific situation in your work or educational experience, or school or community organizations, that illustrates the negative effects of an individual who did not consider the impact of his/her message on the receiver. Send your example to your instructor as an attachment to an email message. Be prepared to discuss your idea with the class or in small groups.

6. Business Writing Can Be Just Plain Awful (Objs. 1–3)

Businesses with better communication standards can communicate more effectively. Yet a staggering number of employees in the corporate world are considered poor writers. Remedies are needed for a multitude of bad writing practices, including millions of vague emails that clog business computers daily, setting off emails asking for clarification that also can't be understood. Review the good writing practices presented in this chapter and locate one or more articles from an online database that addresses writing strategies for business communicators. Begin your research by reading the following article from the Business & Company Resource Center (http://bcrc.swlearning.com) or from another database available from your campus library that provides tips for turning up the power of dull, tedious business writing.

Mackay, H. (2001, April 20). Poor writing in memos and to customers, costs. *The Business Journal*, p. 36.

After conducting your research, complete the following activities designed to raise communication standards as directed by your instructor:

1. Compile a list of mistakes employees make regularly in business writing and speaking. Discuss how failure to correct these problems might affect the business and employees' career potential.

2. Prepare a two- to three-minute presentation that uses a memorable metaphor to describe what you consider to be the three most damaging writing traps. Think outside the box to develop creative, interesting, and relevant content (e.g., apply the lessons of music, theatrics, or a sport to business communication). Be prepared to deliver the presentation in small groups or to the class.

3. Write a "Daily News Alert" discussing one major writing trap. Use an informal but professional writing style that

readers will find fresh and captivating. Include timely research, an interesting anecdote, and/or a memorable analogy that will grab attention and increase retention. Send the message as an email to your class or post it on a class discussion board as directed by your instructor. Monitor the discussion board postings and assess the effectiveness of your message based on the class's response to this daily news alert.

Read | Think | **Write** | Speak | Collaborate

7. The Difference Between a Chuckle and a Boo-Boo in Business Writing (Objs. 1–5)

Locate the following article from the Business & Company Resource Center (http://bcrc.swlearning.com) or another database from your campus library:

Venditti, P. (2003). Express yourself—but make sure it's error free. *Wenatchee Business Journal, 17*(5), C9.

Consider the following questions and prepare a short summary of the article for your instructor.

a. What is the difference between a chuckle and a boo-boo in business writing? Provide other examples of boo-boos in business writing and the consequences.

b. How does Robert Frost's statement "Trying to write without any conventions is like playing tennis without a net" relate to business communication, especially in today's fast-paced technological workplace?

c. Provide at least two writing or speaking errors that make you cringe.

8. Blogging to Promote Business (Objs. 1, 2)

Locate the following article from the Business & Company Resource Center (http://bcrc.swlearning.com) or another database from your campus library:

DeBare, I. (2005, May 5). Tips for effective use of blogs for business. *San Francisco Chronicle*, p. C6.

After reading the article, prepare an engaging flier describing efficient blog use that will be distributed to staff as an electronic attachment to an email.

Read | Think | Write | **Speak** | Collaborate

9. Cultural Barriers to Communication (Objs. 2, 3)

Generate a list of phrases and nonverbal expressions peculiar to your culture that a person from another culture might not understand. Share your ideas with the class in a short presentation.

10. Sensitive Language (Objs. 2, 3)

Interview a person with a disability to find out ways to communicate acceptably using bias-free language. Share your findings with the class in a short presentation.

Read | Think | Write | Speak | **Collaborate**

11. Trickery of Illusions (Obj. 2)

In small groups, select an illusion from the links provided at the text support site (www.thomsonedu.com/bcomm/lehman) or use one provided by your instructor. Allow each member to view the illusion independently and then share his or her individual interpretation with the team. Relate this experience with the concept of perception and its effect on the communication process. Be prepared to share your ideas with the class.

12. Contemporary Language for the Workplace (Objs. 2, 3)

In small groups generate a list of phrases peculiar to your generation that could be confusing and inappropriate for workplace communication. Refer to Merriam-Webster's list of new words for ideas if necessary (http://www.merriamwebstercollegiate.com/info/ new_words. htm). Substitute an expression that would be acceptable for use in a professional setting. Prepare a visual to aid you in presenting your list to the class.

Case Analysis

It's All in the Translation

Business-people frequently communicate by exchanging documents, either printed on paper or transmitted electronically. Those with overseas clients, customers, and contacts can improve their communications dramatically by using software to translate these documents. Such software is used by organizations to produce documents ranging from international correspondence and invoices to complex financial and legal documents.

Growth in the use of the Internet has boosted demand for language translation as users around the world struggle to understand pages in languages other than their own. Multilingual translators allow companies to open up their websites to everyone around the globe. The software determines the country of origin of the viewer, displays the site in the appropriate language, and provides a menu for selecting an alternate language if preferred. Translation packages are typically based on two types of bilingual dictionaries, one for word-for-word translations and another for semantic and idiomatic phrases. Speed of translation is about 20,000 words per hour, with a 90 percent or higher degree of accuracy. Various web-based translation systems are available. Arguably the best known online translation system is Babel Fish, which relies on Systran software to translate pages retrieved by the AltaVista search engine.[22] Language translation software that includes interfaces for text and speech is also available for handheld computers. Users enter words as text and can have the translation returned as text or speech.[23]

Unfortunately, translation systems work best when they are customized for a particular subject area; this involves analyzing typical documents and adding common words and technical terms to the system's dictionary. Using the software to translate Internet pages, which can be about anything at all, often produces dismal results. To make matters worse, most translation systems were designed for use with high-quality documents, whereas many web pages, chat rooms, and email messages involve slang, colloquial language, and ungrammatical constructions. Internet users, however, typically want speed of translation, rather than quality, and are more likely to accept poor results.

It is also possible to use commercial computer-based translation facilities via the telephone, using modems and fax. Messages can be translated using a message translation service for a per-word fee. Although such services may appear costly, imagine the benefit that an organization may derive from conveying an appropriately translated message to a potential client or customer.

In a technological environment that greatly simplifies language translation, some challenges still exist. The problem is often not to translate the words, but to convey ideas across cultures. A writer from the audience's culture may be employed to take translated material and write the ideas in the local language. Experienced practitioners understand the need to consider cultural as well as linguistic differences.

Visit the text support site at www.thomsonedu.com/bcomm/lehman **to link to web resources related to this topic. Respond to one or more of the following activities as directed by your instructor.**

1. Write a one-page summary explaining the factors that have led to the need for more translation services.

2. **GMAT** Write a one-page summary explaining the difference between word translation and culture translation. Give examples of interpretation problems that result when word translation alone is used. Provide instances when word translation would be beneficial to a company.

3. Download a free online translator and translate a sample document such as your personal web page into a target language of your choice. Ask a person who speaks the target language (preferably a native speaker) to evaluate the effectiveness of the translation. Write a one-page summary explaining the quality of the translation. Work in groups if directed by your instructor.

4. Assume that you work for a company that has just entered the Japanese market. Your company wishes to translate correspondence, promotional materials, and invoices into the Japanese language. Using the sites previously listed as starting points, visit four sites of organizations that offer translation and interpretation services. Prepare a two-page written report that (1) compares the services offered by each organization and the accompanying costs, and (2) recommends the one your company should use for its translation services.

5. Research the two software translation programs mentioned in this case. Prepare a chart that summarizes the capabilities and features available with each. Write a recommendation for the superior product.